Sales Training

How to Become the Best Salesman

in Your Industry

By Tony Belfort

Table of Contents

Introduction 3
    Tips for opening a sales conversation successfully 8
Brush Offs – How to Get around Every "It's Not a Convenient Time" 26
Rapport – The Lubricant of the System 34
How to Build Strong Rapport with Your Prospects or Customers to Boost Your Sales 41
Qualification – People Want to Buy Expensive Things 57
Adding Scarcity and Urgency – Never Hear Again "Call Me Tomorrow" 66
Suggesting a Close – Closing Smoothly 83
Dealing with Objections – Please Prove that You Are Telling the Truth 107
Upselling – Getting the Biggest Commission from Every Lead 128
Conclusion 142

Introduction

There are yet many books and outlines that give hints on how to make good sales. To be true, many give good tips and are quite helpful. This book offers simple hints and tips which many salespersons and marketers tend to overlook but are the core for making explosive sales.

I can boastfully assure you that your income will be massively increased and you'll experience a massive increase in sales because of this book. This will be the case especially when you take advantage of the information you are equipped with by this well-researched book. The tips in this book are simple and easy to implement, hence, it is a book for all, regardless of your level of education.

This book was written with just one aim in mind - to help the average salesperson have an upturn in monthly income from their sales. With the simplicity with which this book is written and the practical day to day examples and scenarios that are shared in this piece, you will achieve this target.

This is, however, dependent on the reader. It is important to note that this is a business book, one that is meant to boost sales, and it should, therefore, to be taken as a business guide. The book will be more profitable with this kind of mindset, rather than reading it for a hobby or for leisure. Of course, you can read it during your leisure or free period but the mindset should be with some seriousness.

The reason I advocate reading this book with some serious mindedness is not far-fetched. A while ago, I met a guy at the park, he was holding a book on his left hand and his mobile phone on the other hand. I noticed he was glancing through both alternatively. I was waiting for a friend of mine and after a while, I needed to sit down. I took my seat beside him, which was when I realized the book he was reading is one that I have read myself. It's a book on communication. This book actually helped me to sharpen my communication skills and for some funny reasons, I was quite happy to see him read it.

This prompted me to ask him some questions and start up a conversation with him. You would have thought the conversation will go quite well as I learned to communicate better and he's learning from the same source. To my utmost surprise, it was quite the opposite. He was very bad at communicating the very basic things on his mind. More surprisingly, he flouted every single communication tip that I could remember in the very book he was holding (and supposedly reading).

I had to re-educate him on simple things like starting a conversation and how to keep a conversation flowing. Those were the very core of the book he was holding. Apparently, his girlfriend has been complaining of how bad he is at communicating, and how he's acting very boring in business meetings, how their conversations end so abruptly etc. He, however, didn't see this as a big deal, but every lady needs someone she can talk to and he was nowhere near that person.

The book in his hand was the solution to that problem but he wasn't serious enough with it to learn the principles and become a better communicator. He had read more than half of the book but hadn't learned anything at all.

He was still the same guy, having issues with the world because of his communication skill. Even though she had bought the book to help him improve, it didn't change anything. The problem wasn't the book; the problem was the reader himself.

Take this book with some seriousness, learn the principles that are explained in this work, relate with the examples given, visualize them, and more importantly - practice them, and you'll see how rapid you can make sales.

Intro – How to Open Sales Calls & Meetings

It's true what they say that "first impression lasts longer." It is a principle in psychology called the "primacy effect". It's important to know how to start a conversation with your customers and retain their attention till that point where they are overtly convinced about the product you're selling to them. It's not good enough to start a conversation, if it doesn't end up with the customer buying whatever goods or services you're providing. It is a futile effort. It is therefore pertinent to know how to open a sales conversation.

Tips for opening a sales conversation successfully

1. **Get the prospect's attention:** this is the very first thing to do irrespective of whatever medium you're using, phone call, email or a sales meeting. If you go off trying to make your sale without having their attention, you'll be wasting your time.

2. **Build rapport and make them trust you:** This is arguably the most important part of the sales conversation. A good rapport between a salesperson and a buyer always fares well for the salesman. You must be able to build an understanding with them. Knowing that you're a human being and that you understand their needs, makes it easy

for them to trust you. Never give an impression that all you care about is selling your product. Relate with them in whatever way you can, talk sports, politics, relationships etc. However, in all these, don't compromise your standards; know what you need to know about your products and pass them across in the friendliest and yet stern way possible. Be known for your integrity as well. Nothing buys trust as quickly as integrity. If you promise to call them over the availability of a product, be sure to do so. If you promise to send a mail, don't fail at it. This makes them confident in you. You wouldn't just be winning over a buyer; you could be winning over a family or an association. Be sure that they'll refer you to others if they trust your competence and are certain of your integrity. At this point, they believe almost any price you call for a product without double checking. Of course, this wouldn't happen in a day or at the first meeting, that's why the impressions you give at the first time is very important to buy over the customer beyond that particular day of meeting or the goods being sold. If your customers are not convinced enough to come back and buy from you, you're definitely doing a bad job in sales marketing. Let's talk about how not to lose them at the first time

3. **Know your buyers:** It's important for you to know that people are different. That sounds like a cliché but it's very much important in sales conversation. People don't buy the same kinds of goods, people don't have the same amount of monies in their pockets and people are more willing to do certain things than others. The differences go on and on. It is therefore inappropriate to use the same method or say the same things to everybody. People will get tired of hearing you say the same things time and again. It might work for buyer A and it doesn't work for buyer B. If you want to make consistent sales, you have to sound as unique as possible. This has a lot to do with the interpersonal relationship you build with your customers. You must, of course, realize that your buyers have a life and you're joining in something that has existed long before they met you. Once you realize what's going on in their lives, you can easily know why they need your product or service. This helps you to hit the nail on the head. In telling them how

beneficial the product is to them, hit at that particular spot, your target should be that weakness you figured out. You sound more impressive and convincing if you can tell them why you think they need your product and how it can be beneficial to them. This is why it's very important to pay attention to even the minutest information in the sales conversation. People always tend to say things about themselves very unconsciously, it might even sound very irrelevant to the present conversation or to the sales at hand. But trust me, every single information you gather about your buyer always help in sales conversation. There's always a point when that information comes in handy in sales negotiation. You get to know people simply by listening to them, then you can ask the right questions. The more questions you ask, the more information you have about their situation and the more they are willing to talk.

4. **Be present minded:** Nothing discourages a buyer more than a seller who is physically present at the conversation but is elsewhere mentally. It's okay to have thoughts about what to give your daughter for her birthday or the perfect place to take your wife out for dinner. It's very much

normal to have different thoughts run through your mind, both the good and the bad ones. What is not allowed is to focus on that while you're having a sales conversation. The buyer has to see that you're paying attention to them. This makes them feel valued and respected as a customer. Another thing to consider is the possibility of getting useful information about the buyer without paying ardent attention to them. That's not possible. It's not enough that you have their attention if you can't give them yours. Give a hundred percent attention to them and they will feel honored that you're giving so much to them but in reality, you will get far more from them than whatever time and energy you're giving to them. Look at it as an investment, the returns will mean that they will morally feel compelled to buy from you. It doesn't matter whether you're seeing them physically or talking to them over the phone. What they want to think is that they have your attention, so give them that. I can't imagine a salesperson talking to a customer or prospective buyer over the phone and at the same time physically attending to another one. It's quite bad for you because you might lose both. The one over the phone will especially feel insulted and ignored for someone else because of their physical unavailability. You can't afford this. You must make everyone feel respected. Give them all the time and attention they need.

5. **Ask provocative questions:** the best way to start a conversation is by asking simple questions about stuff that interest the second party. It might or might not relate directly to them. This is the same for sales conversations. Ask the prospects questions but don't sound interrogative. Be tactical. Ask provocative questions that are not directly related to them but will make them say things about themselves. For instance, if it's a lady and you're talking about hairstyling, you could ask a question like this; "many of my female friends and customers tend to prefer wigs and I don't seem to understand why?" this is a subtle way of asking "do you like wigs?" it's more conversational and helps to keep the conversation flowing. You can get an answer like "it's true that many people tend to prefer wig but personally for me..." that's your jackpot! They bring it home to themselves. If you go for the more direct manner of asking the question; "do you like wigs?" you can get

varied answers and none of them will be expressly about them. You might get just a yes or a no. then that's the end of the discussion, you gain nothing useful. If she's meaner or in a less friendly mood, her response might be "it's none of your business." Truly, it's none of your business. It's just natural and more conversational to ask indirect questions to help keep the flow. Let them personalize the question by themselves. Naturally, the longer people talk to you, the freer they become around you. Let them keep talking, you just keep adding one or two things to get them to talk more. It might be a question, a suggestion or an addition to what is said, it could even be an entirely contrary view. But don't get too distracted, remember that the purpose of everything is to win them over to buy your product and as well keep patronizing you.

6. **Have it all planned out:** This is pre-meeting planning. Before getting on the phone or meeting up with a prospective buyer anywhere, you must have planned everything mentally. This always ends at what you plan to achieve with each conversation which is to make sales. Do your research about each person. You should plan what to

say to this person and what not to say to the other etc. This helps you to be more straight forward and gives you a higher chance of success from the conversation.

Many salesmen see sales conversation as different from the usual day-to-day conversation. It's easy to think that since the conversation is all about making money for yourself or selling your product, then that's all there is to discuss. This is the mistake that most salesmen make and it's the same reason customers don't find the conversation convincing to patronize them. Such conversations smirk of selfishness. Many buyers see salespeople as selfish, caring about themselves only and only willing to make a profit for themselves. That's the reason for the reluctance experienced with many buyers. Coming out all gun-blazing about your product before any buyer seems like a good way to convince them but in fact, what it does is piss them off.

Starting a sales conversation with a sales pitch is not really a good idea. Many times it appears you're forcing yourself on the prospect. It is not wrong in itself to pitch during a sales conversation, the problem is when you start the conversation with the pitch. What you tend to do in this case is bombard the prospect with all the necessary and even unnecessary details of what your company does, the product you offer, how excellent the product is or will be for them, its features etc. you don't even give the prospect a chance to try to understand the information you're trying to pass across. Most prospects get lost in between sales pitch. Starting a sales conversation with a pitch is boring for the prospect. I can bet that when you're done pitching, they won't have followed you even midway through your talk. At the end of the day, you won't have had a sales conversation and you won't be making the sale. A sales pitch is not a sales conversation. Pitching is no conversing. A major problem with pitching is that you're talking from your own point of view as a salesman. You don't even know if what you're offering is exactly what the customer wants. This is why pitching is not a good way to start. It is during the conversation that you can figure out what the prospect really want, then you know how to pitch.

There are three avenues that allow a sales conversation;

    i.   Sales call or emails

    ii.   A planned sales meeting

    iii.   A customer walking into the store

The aim of these three avenues for a salesman is the same, to make sales. The first thing to do in each of these cases or scenarios is to start a conversation. Due to the peculiarity and the differences in the three avenues, how you will go about starting a conversation will be slightly different but it is the basic thing to do.

We'll review the different ways to go about opening a sales conversation for each of these avenues.

i. Sales call or emails: Ordinarily, people have a short attention span for unfamiliar phone calls. This means that if you're going to be making a sales call, you'll need to be straight forward and forthcoming. This doesn't in any way mean you should be talkative and not give the client an opportunity to speak. It doesn't also mean you should start with a pitch. There is a way to get the prospect's attention without starting with a pitch. Remember, starting with a pitch is tantamount to pissing them and making them lose interest.
For instance;
Scenario one: pitching
Salesman: Hello, my name is David, am I speaking with Ms. Jane?

Prospect: hello, yes, this is Jane. How can I help you?

Salesman: I am calling from Royalty Fashion House (company name). We have all sorts of dresses and shoes in various shapes and sizes. We can provide you with outfits for all your outings ranging from daily work outfits, to interviews, dinners and galas, weddings, dates etc. ill like to register your interest for us to start supplying you with some of our outfits. You could also come over to our office or store to try out some of our dresses. So what do you say?

Prospect: thanks a lot for the offer, I'll get back to you on that…….. Hangs up.

The problem with this approach is the amount of pressure it puts on the prospects. Rather than allow a natural flow of events in a conversation, what you'll do is give the prospects information and demand immediate commitment from them, putting them under pressure to respond to your bidding. This is why pitching never works. It appears to favor the seller and not the buyer.

The scenario above is the best possible scenario, where the prospect is calm and patient enough to let you finish your pitch and refuse politely. Some people might hang up while you're talking or wait till you're done and frankly tell you "I'm not interested." This can be discouraging for the salesman but it can be avoided.

Scenario two: conversing

Salesman: Hello, my name is David from Royalty Fashion House, am I speaking with Ms. Jane?

Prospect: hello, yes, this is Jane. How can I help you?

Salesman: Hey Jane, did I catch in a good time?

Prospects: yeah, sure. Go ahead.

This is where you get their attention. You must always ensure that you talk from the prospect's point of view. Unlike the scenario above, the prospect might sincerely not see it as a good time to be interrupted from their daily business by a salesman. Make sure you get a set time that they think is convenient for you to call back. For instance;

Salesman: I have an offer for you, I don't know if this is a good time to talk to you about it.

Prospects: no, not really. I'm in the middle of something.

Salesman: so when should I call you back?

Prospect: you can call back in another two hours.

Salesman: okay. Thank you.

Although they refused to talk at the moment, you still have their attention. They have something to anticipate. At the end of the call, the result should be either that they are convinced about your product and are ready to buy or in the worst case scenario, you should set up a meeting with them where you would have the chance to convince them in person.

The same thing applies to the use of emails. It's quite trickier because you won't be getting instant replies. You might be tempted to put all the necessary information in one mail. That's still a sales pitch. You have to be conversational still. For instance;

Scenario one: sales pitch mail

Dear Jane,

Royalty fashion house offers the best outfits, dresses, bags, and shoes for various events and occasions ranging from dinners and galas, to weddings, dates, interviews etc. We have a huge reputation among our clients and are known for the quality of our fashion products. We are hoping you can be a part of our growing customer base. Looking forward to a positive response from you.

Scenario two: conversation starter

Dear Jane,

We at royalty fashion house understands the need for you to appear gorgeous at work and different social events, we have the perfect fit for you. If you'll like to know about our products and services, please don't hesitate to let us know.

You're more likely to get a response for the second mail than the first. The first looks like a regular ad and will be displayed as such. It has nothing to look forward to except the commitment it expects from them. The second mail, on the other hand, will build curiosity, they want to know what you offer, if it's their style and taste etc. Once they respond, you can then provide more information following the flow of the conversation. This means that you would have to email the prospect severally as the conversation continues but the important thing is that you already have a conversation.

ii. A planned sales meeting: meetings like these are most times the aftermath of sales call or emails. The prospect or client will most likely give you the opportunity to talk first. This means you're the one initiating the conversation. Remember the golden rule, never start a sales conversation with a pitch. Below are 3 steps to start a sales conversation;

- Show some familiarity and interest in them

You, as the salesman, are the one with a product to sell. The prospect isn't bothered about having the product that's why you're having this conversation. The first thing you must realize is, the prospect doesn't care about you or your products. They care only about themselves. That's why you can't make the conversation primarily about you or the product (pitching). Instead, make a list of problems that you know the prospects are facing. You don't have to make it too personal to them. Talk like it's a common problem people face (whether or not it is personal to them). Make sure this is one of the first things you say when starting the conversation. Always incorporate this in your opening statements. Immediately, the pay more attention to you, they want to know how you can solve their woes. That's how to make it more about them.

- Talk like an expert. Make them see that you know what you're saying.

It's expected that you're an expert with whatever you sell or whatever service you provide. You must, however, prove this expertise before the prospect. When they see you as someone who knows what they're saying and can get useful or valuable information from you, they will definitely want to listen to you.

- Engage the prospect with questions

This is where the sales conversation starts. The first two steps are to get their attention. Now that you have gotten their attention, you must engage them.

Asking question is a good way to start a conversation. You must ensure you're not asking a yes or no question. That's bad for any conversation. Ask a question that relates to them, for instance, after you have listed the challenges you feel the prospects are facing. You can ask them "is this true for you as well?" or "do you experience similar challenges as well?" they could respond in this manner "we're (I'm) actually experiencing that as well" or "not exactly, our (my) challenges aren't exactly that. What we (I) face is..." You can pick it up from their response and there you go. You have kick-started the conversation.

iii. A customer walking into the store: this is quite easier for the salesman. He's in his own zone. The customers walk in to meet him. He's not having to look for them. For the customer to walk into the store, it means they have a need that they believe can be met in our store. That's where you start from. Remember, it's all about the customers, not you.

Salesman: good afternoon, how can I help you?

Prospect: I'm interested in (product name)

You can kick off the conversation from that point. Whether or not you have their desired product, you can subtly introduce other product during the conversation but you must be careful to not bore them with so many.

Brush Offs – How to Get around Every "It's Not a Convenient Time"

When a buyer tells you that it's not a convenient time to buy your product, it's not because they don't have the money to buy it. The reason is simple; they are not convinced yet. A good salesperson would not throw their hands up in the air and say "oh, ok. Please come back at a convenient time." The truth is there will never be a convenient time. When they give such excuses, its time for you to begin the process of persuasion all over again. A good salesman really doesn't take "no" for an answer.

Normally when a buyer or prospect says "no", the next thing for them is to end the call or meeting. Once this happens, you have totally lost them. It's incumbent on you to ensure that the discussion doesn't end like that. They have made it quite obvious to you, they lack interest, but it's your duty as a salesperson to raise that interest. You have to make them interested in whatever you're offering them. You can do this by asking a simple question. This should be a question that they need to answer extensively. Yes or no questions are a no go area. Let them explain. The reason for this is to keep the conversation flowing, to give you more time to convince them.

"I understand that you don't seem to be interested in this product, what other alternatives would you like to consider?" a question like this one definitely keeps them in the conversation. If you immediately allow them to end the call or the meeting or you allow them to walk out of the store because they don't like what you display, you will lose too many customers, too many sales, and too much money. The goal of asking this question, for instance, might not be because you have an alternative to offer. The product that they just rejected might be the only thing that you have to offer. Asking for what alternative they'll prefer is to prevent them from ending the call or meeting or walking out of the store. As long as you have their attention, you can still make your sales. What you have to do is to convince them. Let them see why they should buy the product they are rejecting.

Now, we'll look at the different ways to convince a buyer or prospective buyer to buy your product or service after they have rejected it earlier.

1. Let them see the product: It's more real to them when they can see the product with their eyes and hold it in their hands. It's no longer an abstract thing. You must have mentioned the features of the product and how it benefits them but they weren't convinced. With the product now in their hands, start off again with that. At this point they

have more of their sense organ with you, they can see, feel and hear. Explain the benefits of the product in their hands extensively. Doing this helps them to value the product more. Holding it in their hands while you sing 'songs of praises' about its benefits makes the product more attractive and creates a desire in them to want to own it.

2. Tackle the incumbent concerns: there are certain general concerns that make people not buy any particular products. You have to understand your prospects and what these concerns are. In having a successful sales conversation (that will lead to a purchase), the salesman must be able to see with the eyes of the buyer. The buyer perspective is important for any salesman to make a sale. People will naturally tend to buy a product as long as it meets certain criteria such as; they need it, it is able to solve a particular problem, they are in good terms with the seller or provider, they don't deem it as expensive and the timing is good enough. Once these criteria are met, anybody will buy the product. In the case where any of these criteria are not fulfilled, it becomes an obstacle that you must be ready to tackle. The most important of these

criteria is whether they need it and how it solves their problem. Determining how to solve these will help in making the sales.

3. Become an artist: Many people can't help but admire a good artwork. An artwork of nature will often paint a reality to us of what things can or maybe like but not necessarily what they are. They remind us of how beautiful life can be and not necessarily what it is now in reality. This is a good skill in having a successful sales conversation. Be the artist, paint a picture to the buyer of how things can be like with your product. They might indeed not be interested in the product that you are selling but they are definitely interested in themselves. Once you realize what their need is, paint a picture of how your product meets the need. Help them visualize it, and your product will become their number one priority. It won't just be meeting their need; it will become their need. Painting this beautiful picture has a lot to do with knowing what their aspirations are. You should be sensitive enough to pick out from your rapport with them, things they like and how they imagine their lives, work or families to be. Whichever one is

relevant to you, pick on it and show them how relevant your goods or products are in helping them achieve their aspirations. It should make for a tempting view. Creating this vision in their mind helps to raise their interest in your product. Making sales is always about what people want for themselves.

4. Offer the prospect a guarantee: ordinarily, this shouldn't be a difficult thing but surprisingly, business owners, salesmen and service providers seem to not be able to do this. It appears more like they are not sure of what they are offering the clients. I must say this categorically if you are not sure of what you are selling or the service you are providing, don't even try to sell it. It's awful not being able to stand by what you are selling to others. Don't become popular for the wrong reasons. Don't be known as the salesman that sells bad products or offer substandard services. You must be able to stand by your product. A good way to stand by your product is to offer guarantees to the clients. It puts their minds at ease. Of course, it's your integrity that's at stake but if you're sure of what you're selling your integrity should remain intact before and after

the sales. It's better than selling something you can't guarantee, that's worse than not having any integrity.

5. Be more persuasive: Persuasion is the strongest tool in the hand of a salesman. If you can't persuade people to change their minds, then you don't have a business with being a salesperson. You might have to use every available resource at your disposal to persuade them to change their minds. Make use of positive reviews about the products from past customers, let them see how beneficial it can be to them, highlight the different features, their uses and how it helps the user. In doing this, make sure you are not perceived as just desperate to sell. Let them see genuineness in your persuasion that it's for their own good. Make them forget that you're just trying to make some money. Make it about them and not about you.

6. Perseverance: this is when you are able to hold on to something irrespective of the opposition. This is something that many salesmen lack. You don't just bulge at the sight or hearing of an objection. You won't make many sales that way and it doesn't portray you as a serious salesman. It's not everybody that will give in to what you have to say at

the first instance. When buyers see how perseverant you are, they know that you are serious about what you are saying. They know you are saying the truth. But when you are not sure of what you are selling, it's easy to give in to an objection. After all, you don't know if it'll work for them. What more? It helps the prospect to see the value in what you are selling and nobody buys any product until they are convinced of its value.

Rapport – The Lubricant of the System

Relationships are built on communication. You only get to understand anybody based on how much you communicate with them. The same thing applies with the buyer to seller relationship. Excellent communication with buyers or prospective buyers builds a lot of interest in the products you trade or the service you provide. There's an old sales adage; "people only buy from people they like". This is still very much true in today's sales world. Once you can get your customers and prospect to like you, you've won yourself a friend who will always be keen to patronize you. The key behind this very business concept is the word 'RAPPORT'.

As a businessman or salesperson, your aim should be to have some level of interest with your clients and buyers or prospects. Having a strong influence on your customer means that they respect your ideas, contributions, suggestions, experience, and advice. You can use this to your advantage. Due to a strong rapport with them, you would be able to influence them because of that fact that you have earned their trust first in communication. This will make them consider you first for all their market decisions. This means that each time money comes out of their pocket into the market, it goes straight to you. The only exceptions will be for products and services that you don't deal with.

The only way you can build a relationship such as this with your customers is because of your rapport with them. A good rapport is an excellent lubricant for strong relationships. Ease of communication allows the customers to trust you more.

As a salesman, you must always be deliberate with building a strong rapport with everyone you meet, not just those you meet because of business or sales conversation. Everywhere you go, you must have a reputation as someone who people finds it easy to relate and communicate with, have a lot of friends. The more you do this, the easier it is for people to patronize you when you get to talk business with them.

Let me paint this fictional scenario to you;

You met two people on a particular day, Alex and Henry. Alex happens to be a cool person, the kind that you just flowed along with nature and you guys got talking about a lot of things beyond the scope of whatever brought you together. You liked the way he talked and you saw the intelligence in how he talked. Obviously, you'll like to know him more and have him as a friend so you guys exchanged contacts.

Henry on the other isn't a very cheerful person. He's not the kind that talked much and he doesn't smile much as well. Although you guys got talking, you really couldn't talk for so long and definitely not beyond whatever brought you together. Whether you exchanged contacts at this point or not is irrelevant.

Days or weeks later, you needed a major renovation of the furniture at your company and they were both into furniture making and are equally very good. Who would you call?

Take a moment to think about that and ask yourself the question, then try to answer it.

Trust me, it's a no-brainer! You'll go for Alex without even thinking of it. The reason is that you already consider him a friend. Remember *"people only buy from people they like"*. Without taking much thought the obvious choice would be Alex because of the kind of rapport you had on the first day and most likely afterward (assuming you still contacted each other, since you exchanged contacts). Henry is as well good but he stands no chance. In fact, it's unlikely that you find out from Henry what he does for a living because you couldn't talk beyond that limited scope of what brought you together. But since you talked a lot with

Alex you're more likely to find out what he does for a living and have it in your mind. He's a friend after all.

That's how rapport works. Not necessarily only for sales conversation but in the little things you do every day, the people you meet and the friends you make. If people find it easy to consider you a friend or something close to that, if they feel easy around you and can talk to you, the higher the chances to boost the sales of your products and make more income.

One skill that salesmen must have is the how of converting friendships to money. That guy you met at the soccer game, the lady you exchanged contacts with at the mall. You must learn to see every single person you meet on this planet (and beyond if you can) as a prospective customer. As a salesman, the aim of making any friend or meeting anybody newly, deep down in your mind, should be towards making more sales. This is not to say that you meet people and you start ranting about your business. Take it slowly. Build that friendship. It's impossible to be friends with someone and not have an idea what they do for a living. People will always ask. Let your friendship grow on its own and tend it towards business. Don't force it, it'll come naturally. Once they can trust you as their friend, they'll patronize you.

I had to go through all of those explanations because people tend to leave business associations as business associations and friends and family have their own space. All associations and relationships should be business associations or prospective business association to their various degrees. Your best customers shouldn't just be aliens or people you have no close relations with beyond sales point. Your close friends, family, wife, kids, siblings, parents should be your customers as well. If your product is not something they can consume or make use of directly e.g. you sell female clothes and they are males, it doesn't mean you abandon them. No, they have female friends that they can refer you to, they have a girlfriend they'll need to take shopping, they have a sister they who would need new clothes for her upcoming birthday. Everyone is a prospective customer. Every single person you know, whether directly or indirectly, whether regular or irregular, consistent or inconsistent, as one of the best or one of the worst, everyone is a prospective customer. Be that business minded.

Back to business conversations

Having established a customer relationship with friends and family, let's talk about the other customers. Those you don't know very closely, that you most likely don't have any previous relationship with. They are the ones you would be spending minutes on the phone with and hours, seated in front of each other with a table in between, trying to convince.

Whether with your family and friends or a prospect who is a total stranger, one common factor in both these relationships is RAPPORT.

How to Build Strong Rapport with Your Prospects or Customers to Boost Your Sales

1. Give them a chance to talk: a lot has been said about this in the earlier parts of this book. But I really can't overemphasize the importance of this. When you do all the talking, you will sound selfish and desperate. In a conversation, both parties are involved. It's not a one-man show. As a matter of fact, I prefer and always recommend that the prospect or customer do more of the talking. When you let them talk, they have the freedom to express themselves. This will allow them to share with you whatever is causing a hindrance or disturbance to them patronizing you and your products. From here you can know what to do, response to give, an argument to make, solutions to offer, in order to convince them. Convincing a customer is easier this way than you just saying whatever comes to your mind. You are more precise, heads on and consequently more accurate.

   Another reason why letting the prospects do more of the talking apart from making you more precise in knowing how to handle them is the feeling it gives them. The mere fact that you took your time to listen to them to help them work out a solution makes them feel very important. It happens with everybody really. There's a feeling we all get when we talk and people around us listen to us. It makes us feel honored, respected and important. This is unlike when everyone just wants their voice to be heard and no one wants to listen. It makes it all the worse when the clients really have something to say but you don't appear interested in listening, you're too busy talking to convince them but in truth, you're losing them. So when you allow the customer or prospect talk, it gives them an impression that you care about their opinion and you respect their point of view. You really should by the way.

2. Be generous with your compliments: it wouldn't be a bad idea to tell that young man how handsome he actually looks. That lady looks gorgeous on her outfit, why not let her know? You should be known for offering compliments. It does a lot of good to how the person relates to you. It makes you very likable, relatable and approachable. By now you should know that these features can only help

boost your sales and not otherwise. You must learn to give people genuine compliments. There's always at least one thing to like about somebody every time. There might be a thousand other things that you don't like at the time but you have to shut your eyes and mouth to that. You have to look from that one thing and let them know you like it. People love to be told good things about them. To them, it mirrors who they are and how people perceive them. For instance, Clarke knows that each time she steps into David's store, he always gives a compliment about how she looks. Because Clarke like everyone else likes to be told good things about her, each time she changes her hairstyle or she wears a new dress, or she does something differently to before, she goes to David's store to hear what he has to say about it. He'll usually compliment her and tell her about his new products or remind her about the old ones she has promised to get. She could go to his store as regularly as every day after she dresses up for the day. People like social acceptance. That is embodied in compliments. Simple compliments like "good morning

Eva, you look amazing", goes a long way to help boost your sales.

3. Empathize with them: this is one part of the job that many salesmen falter at. They usually don't know how to empathize with their customers. Empathy has a lot to do with being an active listener. Everybody loves to know that they're being listened to and are being understood. Empathy is simply the ability to put yourself in other people's shoes to relate with their joy or pain, how they feel in general. When you're able to convince people that you know how they feel (especially if it's a bad feeling), there's a way it relieves them. That someone understands their feelings helps them to think that they are not alone in whatever situation they're in. it gives them the impression that you are listening to them and that you care about them.

In relating with people, empathy would mean that you put yourself away from the picture for that moment and think about them. It shows selflessness. A characteristic that everybody wants to see in others no matter the relationship. As a salesman, if the clients explain to you why they can't buy from you. Maybe because the kind of materials you have at the time is not what they need for their ongoing project, don't desperately try to convince them to buy it like that. That's a bad sign. It is wicked, selfish, and insincere and shows a lack of empathy. It's a fast way to lose your clients too. Show some empathy. Try to understand where they're coming from and then proffer a solution that suits them, not necessarily you. It could mean that you refer them to some other place where they can get what they want or you help them order it and let them get it from you. Being helpful in this way will help win their trust. They will love your selflessness and easily consider you a friend. They'll definitely come back to you for whatever you have. All you have to do to prevent a repeat is to have all the available types of the product that you can lay your hands on. Of course, you must let them know that you know have that same product they couldn't get from you before. Even if they don't need it again, they'll refer orders to you and not where they got theirs from.

4. Use the social media to your advantage: more than half of the world's population are on one social media or the

other. The social media, therefore, has become a large market for any serious sales person to sell their goods. There is a popular belief in the business world that the success of a business organization depends on their social media activity. I actually buy into this idea as well.

The social media affords salesmen the chance to know their clients, customers, and prospects. You can get information about them from their public profile. You can get to know their preferences, things that they like and dislike, you get to know them better. This will aid you in the cause of communicating with them. It's even more likely that they're surprised at how you know so much about them without them telling you, forgetting that they put so much about them online. This will catch their attention and help you create a better rapport with them.

The social media is now a global market. That's where the best brands sell themselves out to people. it gives you a wider reach, a larger connection. A friend of mine runs a coffee shop just along the road downtown. Things were going quite well with him until he started creating and posting different ads for different social media. It's really about packaging your brand. If I didn't know the coffee shop or its owner, I would have thought it's a very big coffee shop. The ads were too good for a coffee shop that small. His business really started booming. People started coming in. they were probably even disappointed at first at how small it was but they came in and like the coffee. Others in the neighborhood who weren't customers saw the bandwagon trooping in and joined in. his business grew quickly. He recently opened another branch of his coffee shop elsewhere that's about thrice the size of the first. Now he's richer and employs more people. How? Social media!

Social media brings you closer to your prospect. For everyone that clicks the "follow" button and every time you click the "accept" button, you stand a chance of growing your business. Always remember that every friend you make, and everyone you meet, it should be with a business aim in mind.

5. Be informal in your conversation: you must make sure you don't sound like you have been programmed to say and do certain things during sales conversations. Be human. Don't be a robot. "Hi Mr. Frankie, what can I do for you this

morning?" this sounds very polite and yet very friendly as well. You should learn to call people by their names. It shows that there's a relationship between you two.

6. Don't knock off competition: this is a very tempting thing to do. Salesmen who talk too much often tend to fall into this trap. After they are done saying all that they can about their product and they think the prospects are still not convinced, they start to rant about how bad the other's products are, what they feel is bad about it. If you continue in this lane, you won't stop at painting the competition bad, you start lying as well. This is not just immoral, it's stupid and childish. Guess what? The prospects will always find you out. They will know that everything you're saying is not because of their own good but for your own selfish interest. It will be obvious how selfish and desperate you are if you can so willingly take down someone else's business and product for just one person to buy yours. If you do this with all your prospects and customers, you'll soon go broke. Every single one of them will avoid you. You will become famous for all the wrong reasons. People will begin to speak badly about how badly you speak of others.

Your competitions will get customers without stress and you'll be left stranded.

You can convince your prospects without saying a thing about your competition. Even if they ask about your competitions' products, it's still wrong to say it's all bad. That's too petty. Tell them the good things about your competition's product and tell them why your product is better for them. Let them draw the comparison for themselves. You'll be a person of integrity this way. It'll be easy to win your prospects over if you don't take the bait of painting others black. Your integrity is kept intact.

7. Accept objections as part of the game: the purpose of this book is not to help you win ALL your prospects. If I said that, I'll be a liar. Whoever tells you it's possible to win over everyone is barely deceiving you. The truth is it's impossible to win over every heart. This book will help you avoid obvious mistakes that the average salesman makes in trying to win over prospects. It'll help you win over clients and keep them but it's not a guarantee that you'll win every single one of them.

You must learn to take objections and rejections as part of the business and use them as assets to get better. One thing I've realized is that in every communication, there's something to learn. You must learn to ask the "why" question. If for instance, you have tried so hard to convince a prospect but they just won't be convinced, you should ask why? Why do they prefer other products to yours? You must ask as politely as possible. Ensure you don't sound demeaning of their preference. Be sincere and polite in asking them why. Let them explain to you, what has caught their fancy. Their rejection of your product is already something to talk about o its own. The longer you get them talking, the more open they get with you, the more they trust you and the more information you can retrieve from them. If they don't find you relatable with, they won't be free enough to open up to you. This is detrimental to your business. Rapport helps to build trust that opens up a chance for more communication.

Once you can extract that from them, you have gained something. You now have another thing added to your list of what to improve on. One thing you have to learn about business is that you're meeting people's needs. So it can't be about you. If it's about you, it can't be about them and if it's about them, it can't be about you. It's their needs to be met. If your product doesn't meet up, you don't expect to get a yes.

Getting a "no" should be an asset for you. So you can appraise yourself, know what to work on, improvements to make and where to invest in. this will help your business grow, have more customers and make more income. Like I said earlier, you can't win over everybody, you can meet the needs of everybody but you have the majority to contend with.

8. Look for other common ground between you: already you know that there is a common ground between you and your prospects already. This is what brought you together. The goods you sell or the service you render already brings you together. But it doesn't necessarily mean it'll create a rapport between you. Always ensure you're not the business as a usual person. In a sales conversation, a little distraction from the topic of discussion is allowed. The customers wouldn't find you friendly enough if all you do is

talk business. They'll find you boring and stereotypical. Always look for another common ground between you both to the thread on. If for instance, your prospect is a nursing mother and you're one as well or you have gone through that stage at some point before. You can talk about your experience bringing up your own child. How troublesome infants can be and how often you had to breastfeed him. This already creates some closeness with the prospects. It makes it feel like you're already a part of what they are going through. If you're a male in the same situation, look for some other common ground. You can use the same as well if your wife is a nursing mother or she's been through that path. Show some empathy. Tell her about the things that your wife had to put up with during that period. If you're single and you know nothing about it, you can ask questions. E.g. how do you cope with being a nursing mother as well as a businesswoman?

You should learn to ask questions while discussing such common ground issues. It builds the rapport. The more they talk about themselves the more easily they feel around you. This is a key factor in making friends, as well as nailing down sales.

One thing you must be very cautious about is when to switch to the sales conversation. This is relative to different prospects or customers. Some people might be willing to talk to you for as long as you can listen while some others just want to do business and leave. Some might be willing to chit chat but for not too long. You must be able to read each person differently. Know when to deviate from business when you want to. Know when to go back to business as well.

9. Be polite and humorous: humor works a lot in sales conversations. Your ability to make your clients smile regularly and the frequency of your laughs and smile shows you're good at communicating what's on your mind to others. Prospects will always see you as someone who can offer good customer service. If you approach a prospect with a smile and with lots of humor, they'll respond to you similarly and you can kick off your rapport from there. A humorous person will very easily be approachable because they'll be seen as friendly. I once heard a story of a lady

who always goes to a particular grocery store simply because the guy there always makes her smile. At times she goes to the store, not because she needs anything she's going to buy, rather she's going there so he can put a smile on her face. She claimed that she goes to the store whenever she's sad and angry and she never comes out the same way. As a business minded person, you should know that she never goes into the store and comes out empty handed. She goes in sad but comes out happy. Howbeit, not without buying certain things whether or not she needs it.

This is the power of humor. It's a very effective tool in building business relationships. You must, however, realize that it doesn't replace politeness. Being rude will take away the shine in your humor. Once people sense you as rude, it dampens their sense of humor and it becomes more difficult for you to communicate with them on that level. You definitely need the right blend of humor and politeness.

10. Practice the principle of reciprocation: customers will find it easier to keep discussion when they know that you're

following and listening attentively. As a salesman, you can't but be listening to whatever your prospects or customers are saying at any time. I must say that nothing can be quite as annoying as having said a lot of things only to discover that you have not communicated with anybody because the audience was somewhere else in mind. One very important way of assuring your prospects or customers that you're actively listening to and following them is to be reciprocation. If they smile at you, make it a point of duty to smile back. If they lean toward you, lean forward towards them as well. This does not mean that you're mimicking them, it means that they have your attention. It can be unconsciously done but you can make sure that you do it deliberately.

11. Follow up on previous discussions: you can ask a question in this regard. If you talked with a customer or prospect previously about something, bringing it up again the next time you see them or hear from them always excites them. It gives them the impression that you listened to them very well enough, it makes them think that you care so much about them to not forget what they told you about.

Take, for instance, a prospect discussed with you a week or two previously about the possibility that they take their kids for a summer holiday trip. If you get to see them later or you had to call them for certain reasons, it will be a good idea to ask about the trip. Whether or not they have gone. If they have gone, ask how it went, if the kids had fun, if they really enjoyed the trip, how they reacted and what the experience was like for them and the kids generally. If they haven't gone, ask about how their plans have been coming up, if they were still going or not, if they've got everything they need ready. You may offer advice and tips that you feel are helpful to their cause.

Asking these questions about a two-week-old conversation that was probably mentioned slightly, shows genuineness and selflessness. It shows that you care, they'll find you friendlier and would easily relate with you on other days about other issues. This, in essence, means that you'll win their trust simply by asking to follow up questions on previous discussions.

The importance of a good rapport with your prospects or existing customer cannot be overemphasized. Having a good rapport with clients and people generally increases your chances of making more sales.

Qualification – People Want to Buy Expensive Things

There are very important things that you must determine in the course of your conversation. Asking questions is usually the best way to drive conversations. As a salesman, you must be able to direct your questions to particular things. You must be able to extract from the prospects particular issues that they are going through that you (or your product) can help them solve, you must be able to extract from the conversation their desire, degree of urgency, level of income, spending ability etc. this helps you to know whether or not the prospect is worth pursuing. Not all prospects are worth the time, energy and resources that the average salesman puts into convincing them. It's a sad thing to spend a considerable amount of minutes, or hours or days and weeks trying to convince a prospect only to find out that he doesn't have the budget or spending power to purchase the product. It's a total waste of time, energy and resources and worse still, it deprives you of spending quality time with other prospects more deserving of it.

To be effective in your sales conversation, there are at least 6 things that you must extract from your prospects during the conversation;

- budget or spending power

- authority to make a decision
- revenue generation over time
- the time frame for the sale
- alternatives and requirements.

Budget or spending power:

Like I stated earlier, this is a very important part of the conversation. It is something that you must know early enough into the conversation. Before you sing all sorts of songs and say all sorts of things to try to convince the prospects, before you even start to pitch, you should have a pretty much idea whether or not the prospect can afford your product or service. This is to prevent you from spending unnecessary time on prospects that are not suitable for your market and are more unlikely to buy. This might seem like a something a little bit difficult to determine but it's not really difficult. A lot of people are actually comfortable with the idea of telling you how much they intend to spend. This will save you both a lot of stress. Once you have an idea of what they want and you're sure you can provide the product or service, give them a range of price to determine their budget. For example: "I understand why you need this product and I know how important this is to you. The price is however between $800 - $1000. I'm sure that fits well into your budget, right?" depending on how you perceive the client to be, you can be more straight forward about it. "The price for the product is around $1000." There are only one of two responses that you can get. Its either they agree. "That's about right with me." Or they say "that's way more than I can afford". At this point, you know where the discussion is heading. For the second response, you can press further (if you can afford to) and ask "how much can you afford?"

Revenue generation over time:

Not all prospects will become buyers and not all buyers will become regular customers. Some people are only considering you and your product for short term reasons and don't intend coming back after that. One time buyers aren't worth pursuing. You should spend more of your time with prospects that are more likely to become regular buyers than people that will buy once and never again. Staying with prospects that will become regular buyers is a worthwhile investment. You'll generate more income from regular transactions with them. The first sale with them might not yield much profit but you must be able to estimate their worth in the long run. After you've gained their trust, they'll be more regular and be willing to pay more for your product because of the trust they have in you. They might even refer others to you for free. Depending on the kind of goods you sell or the service you offer, you should be able to determine this with your customers. These are the people you invest your time and resources on not one time buyers that just comes and goes.

The timeframe for making the sale

Not all prospects are immediate buyers. You must be able to determine the urgency of your product or service early enough during the sales process. This will help you to know how much time to invest with the prospect and when you should invest such time. You can't waste 6 hours talking to a prospect that won't be needing your product in another 4 to 5 months.

Questions like this "how soon do you want the product delivered to you?" can go a long way to establish the urgency of the need. They might respond with "as soon as possible" or "I'll like to have it in 3 days' time" worse still, they might say "I won't be needing it in another 4-5 months." This last response doesn't mean you should end the call or meeting abruptly and not follow up on them. That'll be rude and you might be losing long term buyer. Plus, you'll always need the money whenever it comes, now or 5 months' time.

What it means is that they can't be your priority for the time being. Focus on making more urgent sales while carrying the long term sale along by following up on them constantly.

Authority to make the purchase

Not all of your prospects actually have the authority to single-handedly make the purchase. Some are representing their companies and are only a lowly member of a hierarchical multi-level decision-making system. Rather than spend so much time with such people, why not ask them subtly if they have the power to call the shots?

"What is the process like in finalizing a deal at your company?" a question like this can easily give you a clue as to how complicated the sales process can be. Investing so much of your time with someone so far below the decision-making system is tantamount to a waste of your invested time and effort. You should try to seek direct contact with the decision maker(s) and then invest your energies in convincing them. If you can't get access to the top bosses. It's a huge risk staying on the deal, you might as well walk away.

Alternatives

This is about knowing what other options they are considering. If they are contemplating or have decided to not go with your product, it's not likely that they are not ready to buy it. It's possible that they have a better offer from your competitor.

For instance, if they are not interested in any of the car you have up for sale, you can ask "do you intend to keep hopping on a taxi?" their answer might give them away as to their next line of action. Whether they're considering an offer from a competitor. If that's the case, you might need to be a little bit flexible, enough to accommodate them to make the sale.

Requirements

This is basically about finding out if your prospect is qualified to buy your product or service. This is very important if you have products or provide services with legal restrictions. If the law dictates that a buyer should be a certain number of years old in order to qualify for the product, then you need to ask for their age. If the company requires a license by the law to use your products, you definitely should ask them if they have the required license to make a deal.

Depending on the flow of the conversation, you can be more direct in asking for the prospect age than asking if they are a licensed company.

"I understand your interest in this product but I'll like to know if you meet the required age to buy one". That's basically asking "how old are you?"

"Due to legal restrictions on ownership of this products or beneficiary of this service, you'll require a license for us to complete this deal". This is a good way to ask "are you a licensed company?"

There are questions that typically sound demeaning and insulting to people, even if you didn't, mean to insult them. Asking a question like "are you a licensed company?" might sound ridiculous. It might appear that you're questioning their credibility. That can piss them off and they'll call off the deal and you lose. It's the same way asking a 22-year-old guy "how old are you, are you up to 18?" that's an insult to his person.

As a salesperson, you must learn when to and how to ask questions if you're going to pull off most of your deals. Like the above instances, there are questions that you shouldn't ask directly unless you're not interested in making the sales (why wouldn't you anyway?). Such questions are better phrased as sentences or observations. You'll get your answer from their response and you wouldn't be feeling insulted by your question.

This tactic is mainly used for sensitive issues like the one above or if you sense that your prospect is feeling uncomfortable being asked a lot of questions. It's a useful tactic but isn't the first choice for all conversation. Questions mostly drive the conversation. However, you must stay away from the "why" question.

Asking "why" many times sounds like an accusation. It makes the prospect feel like they're being interrogated and they feel uneasy. You can ask "what" and/or "how" questions.

Adding Scarcity and Urgency – Never Hear Again "Call Me Tomorrow"

This is a very useful tactic to increase the sales of your products. The scarcity of goods always gives customers a sense of urgency in making a purchase. The fact that they know or perceive that the product is in limited supply would make them hurry in making their purchase so that they are not left to miss out on the product. Adding time constraints to the availability is a tested way of boosting sales.

The effectiveness of this tactics is the fact that people would always buy because they see others buying. They assume that the limited number of products means that it will finish if they don't hurry. This is the same urgency they carry to their workplaces, homes, associations to inform them about this "wonderful product in limited supply". Many end up buying the products not necessarily because they already need it. They buy it because they think they might need it in the future and it might not be available at the time. Whatever their thought is, you're making your sales.

"Opportunities appears more valuable to us when they are less available." This is a principle in psychology known as the scarcity principle. The harder it is to come by something, the more we crave for it. Customers generally tend to associate a small quantity with high quality. People would often think that if it's not so

valuable, it shouldn't be that scarce. Scarcity has always been associated with highly sensitive products. This is how many people determine whether they have spent rightly on quality products or not.

Scarcity refers to placing a limit on the amount of product supplied or a service rendered with the view of putting the customers or final consumers under pressure to buy. The goal behind creating scarcity is for the customers to feel the pressure and ultimate to boost sales of the particular product. Scarcity always creates a sense of urgency in the buyers. It is an effective way to boost sales rapidly.

The urgency that comes with scarcity is the reason why scarcity works. People who are known to sit on the fence about a particular product would be moved to make a quick decision. For instance, you most probably would have tried convincing a customer about a particular product without any luck. They might have appeared unconvinced or even very skeptical about the product. The moment they discover that it is already I'm short supply, you'll definitely notice a change in their appraisal of the product. They start having second thoughts, positive ones this time. The longer the scarcity, the more urgent people see the need for the product. Scarcity forces people to act immediately.

It's very easy for a customer to say "I don't need this now, I'll get it later." Or "I can't afford this right now. I'll come back when I get enough money." Customers find it very easy to brush off salesmen and different products when they think they are in charge and can buy whatever they want, whenever they want it. Scarcity restores that balance. It takes the power from the buyer to the seller. Like a miracle, the products that they didn't want a few days ago become a need for them. They'll be willing to pay more for the same product that they claimed they can't afford. That's the power of scarcity and urgency.

Nobody likes to hear the statement "out of stock". That's why when a product becomes scarce, people do all they can to ensure that they have their share of the remaining lots before it's out of stock.

Creating urgency about a product in a sales conversation is a good way to motivate them to make quick decisions. You don't have to dwell on it too much so it doesn't sound fake. When you hammer too much on it, they will quickly realize that it's fake and you're just trying to trick them into buying. Once you can capture their interest in the product, just mention it to them subtly. Make sure you're not sounding desperate. Sound a lot like you're trying to help them so they don't miss out on the product.

There are different ways to create urgency based on scarcity

1. Set deadlines for the product sales (give a limited time offer for sales of particular products): this type of urgent is based on time. A deadline always signifies the end of a period. When people see a deadline about a product or service that you're offering. It consciously or subconsciously rings a bell in them about how useful the particular product is or can be to them. They might not have the same perception about the product earlier. But scarcity doesn't just create a sense of urgency. It also creates a sense of need. As a matter of fact, the sense of need is what drives the urgency to buy them. There's always a rush that tends to happen towards the end of a deadline. As the deadline edges closer, the urgency increases. People tend to clamor more for it. This strategy works a lot with discounts. Closing the sale at the end of the deadline should be at your discretion. You can choose to extend it and shout it loud for all to know that the sales

deadline has been extended. They'll thank you for the extension but it's you who continues to make your sales.

I know a dude who became a very fond of playing an online strategy game. The game actually requires that you make some in-app purchases to enjoy it better. But he got on with the game really well without making any of the game purchases because he felt the prices for the purchases were too expensive for him to invest in a game. This continued till they made an offer. They offered a discount for different purchases in the game. It was at this point that he realized how much he has been left behind by other players of the same game constantly making those purchases. He never considered the necessity of this purchase before that time. It never occurred to him that he was being left behind in the game. It never occurred to him that he needed the purchase to boost his chances in the game. On seeing that one time offer and the deadline that was set for it. He had a sudden sense of need and urgency sets in. he did everything possible for him to ensure he was not left out of the discounted one time offer. He ended up making the purchase.

That is the power of time driven urgency. People start considering things they never considered before. I'm sure that there are other players of the game that would have made the purchase not because they thought they needed it like my friend but because it was an offer and the clocking was ticking on it.

According to psychologists, this tactic works effectively due to the principle of loss aversion. The loss aversion theory states that the pain of losing something is psychological twice the pleasure of gaining something. This means that humans feel twice as much pain when they lose something than the pleasure they get from gaining anything. This principle is what drives people to buy sales limited products. They are trying to avoid the pain of losing such an opportunity.

2. Add countdown for prices: this is similar to the product sales countdown. It is also a time-bound scarcity. This tactic makes use of a reduction in the price of products to motivate people to buy within a small time scale. A popular

example of this is the Black Friday sales by different online stores, where you have all their products at much-discounted rates within a 24-hour time limit. This creates a serious sense of urgency in the buyers. If they are going to buy, they must buy now! When people see the countdown, they get desperate to get the deal off.

This also works based on the loss aversion principle. Another psychological principle at work here is what is called FOMO – Fear of Missing Out.

FOMO was clearly defined as "the fearful attitude towards the possibility of failing to exhaust available opportunities and missing out on the expected joy associated with succeeding in doing so."

Nobody likes to miss out in anything good. This is why FOMO and loss aversion becomes

very effective in making the buyer buy and making more income for the salesman.

These principles make it quite apparent that many people buy things not just for the pleasure they derive in it but also because of the fear of losing out on it.

3. Holiday or seasonal offers: this tactic is what you put up during a holiday or an especially celebrated event. You must have seen many of the summer bonuses, Christmas offers, independent day discounts etc. those are seasonal offers that have urgency by themselves. This is because the holidays don't last forever. Already there's a natural time-bound offer in this tactic. You can make this time bound offer more effective by adding the countdown.

Many people are so used to the clockwise, increasing movement of the clock that it doesn't create so much urgency like when they see the clock counting backward and reducing. Countdowns give people this *"there is no time"* mentality and it effectively creates more urgency than running late to catch an 8.am bus.

A season like the Christmas season only comes once towards the end of every year and it is widely celebrated. Giving out offers during this season helps to boost sales. In the spirit of the fanfare, people buy a lot of things, both needful and needless. Giving an offer during this will be effectively proverbially "using two stones to kill one bird." Tell the customer that the bonuses and discounts are your own way of saying thank you for the year. They tend to appreciate such a gesture. They are more likely going to use the opportunity of the ongoing offer to order for more than usual. The same way every salesman wants to maximize their profits, buyers want to minimize their spending. This is the psychological advantage of giving regular promos and offers. People buy more during these periods in order to minimize their spending later. Hence the urgency they have. The regularity of your promos, especially for your most loyal customers, will many times attract more customers to your business with the hope of being a beneficiary of the next promo. Before you know it, you have made a life-long customer.

4. Use urgent words in your conversation: so much has been said about creating scarcity but you can bring it down to conversations too. From speaking to customers, prospects or clients, you can make them realize the importance of acting immediately with the words that you use. When you're trying to convince them about a particular product, like it has been mentioned earlier, creating scarcity helps

them to make up their mind quickly enough. Make it sound like you're concerned about them missing out on the limited number of stocks you have left. Always ensure that in a sales conversation your tone should be towards the prospects or customer. You don't want to give them the impression that you're just trying to make sales at all cost. Let them rather think that if they walk out of your store or end the call with you without already buying the products or booking for at least one of it, they might never get the chance to buy it again. At least not at the price that you're offering them. Don't say this directly to them, it might piss them off but make sure that you imply it subtly and very friendly way. Let them know you have their interest at heart. Of course, you must have made them realize the importance of the product to them before creating the scarcity. Creating that scarcity should be your final straw. Say it as you mean it but say it with a "by the way" gesture. This means that you don't start and end a sales conversation with creating scarcity about all your products. That's desperate. The scarcity should be by the way. Say it at the point where they have begun to consider whether to buy it or not. There are certain words that naturally depict urgency. For example, quick, instant, instantly, deadline, hurry, now etc.

Use these words subtly in between your conversations. You don't have to use all at the same time, that's comical. One or two is enough, then you keep quiet about it. You just sow the seed of urgency in them and leave them to make their decision.

Below are two scenarios of a salesman trying to create urgency in the sales conversation. Follow along;

Scenario one:

Salesman (s): …I don't think you understand my point here. I am saying that we have **a limited** production and if you don't buy it **now**. You will lose out on it. (Obviously hammering on the scarcity he tried to create).

Customer (c): I really do understand you but I don't think I should buy it right now. I can always come back for it.

Salesman: by the time you come back, the produce would most likely have been **sold out**. We have a lot of people demanding it. If you have to come back for it tomorrow, it might be unavailable. There's really nothing stopping you from buying it **right now**. You have your credit card with you as well as enough cash to purchase it. You can easily pay for it and get it **immediately**.

Customer: (already getting pissed). Thanks but I'll pass. Why are you so insistent on me buying this thing?

Salesman: The offer **closes** in a few days and we already have **a limited number** of them. It would have been really nice if you bought one of them. So you're really going to pass this chance up?

Customer: thanks but I'm fine. Have a good day. (Customer walks out or hangs up).

Salesman: you too sir.

Scenario two:

Customer: I love it, I just don't think I can afford it right now.

Salesman: smiling…. It's alright. That's not a problem, I understand.

Customer: you said it can … (highlighting the features and benefits of the products).

Salesman: definitely, it affords you the opportunity to... (Highlighting the benefit of the product to the customer). By the way, we have just 3 of it left.

Customer: (thinking on the features and benefits) how much did you say it is again?

Jackpot! The salesman mentions the price and makes the sale.

I'm sure you can easily spot the difference between these two scenarios.

The first salesman was very desperate to make the sale and it made the customer suspicious. You'll also notice that he used words that depicted urgency (words that are darkened in the conversation) quite a number of time. It makes it obvious that there's no urgency, he's only trying too desperately to make sales. Of course, this is what buyers and prospects think typically of salesmen, self-seeking and caring only about making money. The way in which he tried to force money off the customer really is selfish. Such customers wouldn't tell you how pissed off they were but you'll never see them or hear from them again. How do you expect to? You could have as well pointed a gun to their foreheads to convince them to buy your product. The way the conversation ended, it was obvious that the salesman didn't just lose the sale, he lost the man. Your customers are humans too, they expect some empathy from you. They can as well tell when you are watching out for them or you're just desperate to make money.

The second sales, on the other hand, played his game perfectly well. You'll notice that he didn't even use any of the urgency depicting words. Yet he was more successful in planting urgency into the thinking process of the customer. Empathy plays a very important role. Statements like "I understand what you mean" can be underestimated but they mean a lot to the customers. The calmness with which the salesman talked too was crucial to making the sale. Notice that the first salesman practically did all the talking, leaving the customer with no choice than to rather accept or object and the choice was pretty obvious. The second salesman however did little talking and even smiled when he was rejected. The best time to show empathy is when the customer rejects your offer. People are always inclined to reciprocate whatever gestures they receive. When you make them easily realize that you understand what they are saying and you relate well with it. What they do unconsciously is to reciprocate. The try to put themselves in your shoes. They try to see why you want them to buy the product. It is because they have reciprocated your empathy that's why they ask again for the price of a product they already rejected earlier. They begin to make compromises. This is the perfect time for you to create that scarcity. The moment they begin to consider buying it, tell them it limited. When you tell them we have just 3 left in stock or the offer closes tomorrow. What they hear is, if you're ever going to buy it, now is the time. They begin to see more reasons why you have been persuading them to buy it. It suddenly dawns on them how important the product is to their life. The price no longer becomes an issue. You win their trust more and might just have won over a lifelong customer.

The second scenario explained above is how to win over a customer by adding scarcity and urgency. Both scenarios demonstrated above is not necessarily how every sales conversation will go. They were only used to buttress the points above. They might as well serve as a template for how you can pattern your sales conversation. One thing you must always know is that you, as the salesman, are the driver of the conversation. It only ends up wherever you drive it. That's why you require skillfulness in communicating effectively with your customers.

Suggesting a Close – Closing Smoothly

Closing a sale is the high point of any sales conversation. This is where you want all time, energy, resource and talks to end up at. If you talk for so long and it doesn't end up at closing a sale, it might as well have been a waste of time. This is the crux of sales meetings. This is the reason why you keep calling prospects, meeting with them to discuss, spend a lot of time trying to convince them to buy that good, it's all in a bid to close a sale.

Closing a sale would generally refer to when the clients finally make the decision to buy your product or make the purchase. It is usually the end of the sales process.

Only one out of ten prospects might be willing to close the sales by themselves. This implies that the duty of closing the sales falls majorly on the salesman. Many salesmen especially amateurs and newbies find it difficult to close a deal. The truth is, there's always an air of nervousness when the salesman gets to the point where he would close the sale. This is mainly because he doesn't know what to expect from the prospects. The possibility of rejection always rings true in the heads and minds of many salesmen, that's why they are very poorly at closing deals.

Closing a deal is a very vital part of the sales conversation. While I can't say it's the easiest part, it definitely is not the hardest part of the sales conversation. It really shouldn't be a big deal for a good salesman especially if he has done his homework well during the sales process. Closing the deal might be as simple as making just one statement or in many cases, just a suggestion. While in other cases, it might be as difficult as going over the whole sales process again.

Any salesman worth his salt would be able to tell at the end of his sales presentation or conversation if the prospect is ready and willing to make the purchase. Just observing the prospect's body language and being attentive during the sales conversation is helpful in determining whether the prospect is convinced enough to buy or not. I don't recommend that any salesman suggests closing the deal if they aren't convinced that the prospect is convinced. Suggesting a close to the deal when you know that the prospect is not convinced is more likely to complicate the deal and leaves the salesman more susceptible to rejection.

Suggesting a close during sales conversation should be the last on the agenda of things to do. You should only go for it after you are certain. The way I see closing a deal is similar to something you have just one shot at. You know you can't miss your target. It's like when you go game hunting, whether you go with just one bullet in your gun or with whole ammunition if bullets like a soldier preparing for war, you only have one shot at the game. If you miss your shot with just one bullet, that's the end of hunting for the day. Likewise, if you have whole ammunition with you. If you miss the first shot, you're tempted to keep firing but the likelihood for success becomes thinner with every shot. You're more likely to not hit the game, as well as scare others into hiding with repetitive shots.

Either way, unless you get the first shot right, whether, with a single bullet or hundreds of bullets, you're likely to go back home empty-handed.

This scenario applies to the sales process. You're the hunter, your prospect is the game, suggesting a close is a bullet. You only have one shot. You should only use it when you're a hundred percent certain of its success. Suggesting a close repetitively increases your chances of failure to close the deal. It pushes the clients to a corner and makes them go on the defensive. It makes it look like you're forcing the product on them and gives them more reasons to say no. this is why the single shot scenario becomes important.

By now you already have a question on your mind. When you want to close a deal and you are not sure if the prospect is convinced or not, what should you do?

In this case, you simply ask the question to ascertain how convinced they are about the deal. You should only make the move after you have confirmed this. Questions like this should help;

How do you feel about our services or about the product now?

I believe you now understand how important this product is to you?

You can as well imply a question in a suggestive manner like this;

By now you must be convinced about the usefulness and importance or our product or service

Asking these questions or implying it in this manner will prompt a response from their part. There are only three types of responses that you can get at this point, it's either positive, negative or neutral. This will help you to know if they are already convinced about your product or service.

Positive means they are totally convinced about the product and are ready to buy. Once you can get a response like this, then its time to push for the close.

Negative means that they are nowhere near being convinced and are certainly not buying. They might not even have any interest at all. You'll be making issues more complicated if you push for the close after this. What you should rather do is to sit down and rethink your sales strategy.

Neutral means they might be interested but they still have certain objections about it. I call it neutral because it connotes both the positive and the negative. However, it is more positive than negative. Making a sale or pushing for the close after getting a neutral response depends a lot on you, the salesman. That's what makes it more positive than negative. It is left for you to answer all their questions and quell all their objections. If you can successfully do this, which you should, it becomes positive and you can suggest a close. If you fail at it, however, it becomes negative and that's the end of the deal.

For instance;

Response 1: I now fully understand the importance of what you offer, I believe your services are very well suited for our company.

Response 2: I understand what you mean except that I have a little issue believing that this medication cures cancerous cells.

Response 3: I must commend your effort in trying to convince me but I just don't see how this product is of any use to me.

If I was a teacher, I would have asked you to match the three responses to their different classes (positive, negative or neutral). But that can't be farfetched, response 1 is positive, response 2 is neutral while response 3 is negative. From these responses, you know what to do. Whether to shoot your shot or back off completely. Remember, you only have one shot at it.

Types of closing techniques

Closing a sale for some salesmen have become naturally instinctive. However, this is not true for all salesmen. Due to the importance of closing a deal and its determinant as to whether all the sales man's labor will be crowned with a sale, salesmen have come up with different techniques that can be useful in different situations to close a deal. The aim of closing techniques is to reduce the resistance from the prospect and put them in a position to buy.

1. **Assumptive close:** this close technique depends a lot on the salesman. The salesman is the one driving the sales process. It

works based on the assumption that the prospect is ready to buy your product. This means that having gone through all the sales process, the salesman is confident that the prospect is convinced about the product and subsequently assumes that they are ready to buy. This is the most important and most used sales technique. In suggesting this type of close, it could be with a question or an affirmative statement that suggest the deal has been completed. For instance,

- So Mr. X, how many units would you like to be in the first batch of supplies?

The above question already assumes that Mr. X has no objections and is ready to buy the product. To assume that confidently means you have done a great job in quelling all his objections during the sales process. This technique is based on positivity and the prospect will likely respond in the same vein. You can suggest this technique in form of a statement if the customer isn't one interested in many questions. For instance;

- I can send over the first batch of supplies to you as early as tomorrow.

This statement assumes already sounds like he's paid for the product and all that's left is delivery. The prospect definitely won't think otherwise.

2. **The urgency close (now or never close):** one situation where the sales technique becomes useful is in a situation where the prospect wants to buy but for some unreasonable reasons they aren't going for it. Closing techniques help them to make that decision. In this situation, the urgency close comes in very handy. This technique invokes time and creates a sense of urgency in the prospects. This technique is a very effective technique when it is being used but it is not the everyday technique. It's the kind of technique that you only sparingly, use once in a while, otherwise, you lose your credibility. There is no obvious lie than invoking time to sell all of your goods. The prospects will find you out.

Examples;

- We've been selling at a discounted price and the offer is ending tonight.
- You're quite lucky cos we only have one piece left at that price.
- The demand for it is high, and the price keeps increasing with each shipment.

This technique gives the prospect less time to think or seek for other alternatives. They know they have to make the decision as soon as possible. The fear of losing out would often make them go for the purchase.

3. **The take away close:** this technique has a lot to do with the customer or prospect's psychology. It's a psychological practice that is useful when the prospect seems to like the product but for some unreasonable reasons are holding back. It easily breaks that inertia and forces them to make a decision immediately. It is similar to taking away a particular thing, maybe a toy, from a kid. There's a way that the fact that you have taken that thing from them makes them want it all the more. That's how it is in this case too. For instance, this technique can be used in a case where you have explained all the features and the benefits of the product to them but they still appear to be holding back largely because of the price. What this technique suggests is taking away a feature from the product or service and offering it to them again at a discounted price.

For instance;

Since you think $200 is too much, how about I take away the (particular feature), then you can have it for $155. That's fair enough right?

Saying this already takes their mind off the $200 price tag, they begin to think of buying the product without the particular feature and it doesn't always sit well with anybody. They feel that the feature you excluded is the most important part of the product and as such, they have to get the product with the complete feature. They begin to think less about the $200 and begin to weigh the $45 difference.

They will practically want the removed feature more than the whole product and they begin to think of the difference as affordable. They could think along this line for instance;

$45 for that feature is definitely affordable, I'll have to go for it. So they add up the $45 you removed back to the last $155 to get their desired product and you sell the product at your desired price and everybody is happy!

4. **Hard close:** this is a riskier closing technique. It's unlike the other techniques in many ways. It's not an everyday technique to close a deal. Only use it when you have nothing to lose. The hard close requires a whole lot of confidence from the salesman. If you

have tried convincing your customer on all fronts and they still object to buying. You must be able to ask yourself if you're willing to do business with that particular person again. If you still intend to do business with them in the future or you need the links and referrals that they can provide, NEVER use the hard close on them. It is one of the fastest ways to destroy seller to buyer relationships. That's why it's advisable to be used as a last resort and only when you have nothing to gain from the customer again. This means it's likely just a one-time sales deal with them and you have nothing to lose. This technique is not for everybody and should only be used by established, skilled and experienced sales professionals. The technique usually creates unpleasant emotions for the customers like anger, resentment, stress etc. and there are only two ways they can react to this. If the prospects manage their stress and emotions well enough, they might still say no. if you get a "no" that spells an end to any form of business relationship between you both. However, if they feel under pressure and show a lack of confidence in their decision-making ability, this is a good sign for you. You need to respond with a trial close. You can ask a simple question like "what do you think?" this tends to reduce the pressure and stress on them and they ultimately will go for the buy. This technique utilizes a lot of confidence. The man with the most confidence always wins.

5. **Summary close:** this is a very commonly used technique as well. Haven gone through the rigors of the sales process, the calls, emails, meetings, everything you said to try to convince them to buy. It actually makes sense to go over them again. Summarizing the benefits and features of the product in a few sentences gives them a clearer view of what they are about to buy. This draws their attention to the product. It helps them to visualize exactly what they are buying and makes it easier for them to go for it. This technique is similar to the agricultural practice of taking away the weeds so that the plants can stand out and grow more. By summarizing everything said about the product during the sales process in a concise manner, you're making the picture clearer and the product desirable to the client. For instance, you can say something like this;

"here you have a washing machine that is portable enough to fit into a very small space and washes dries and presses your clothes in less than 5 minutes."

6. **The puppy close:** this technique is useful for salesmen who have the luxury of allowing their prospects to take their goods or

products home to try out. The longer time they spend with the product the more affection they develop for the product. It's like giving a dog lover a puppy to take home for a week and decide whether to buy it after a week. The probability that they would buy the puppy after a week is over 90%. People tend to grow an affinity for something that they feel they own. This close can't be used by all salesmen because not all products can be taken away to be tried out first before they are bought. An example of those that can use this technique is the used auto sales professional. You can allow the prospect to take the car away for a week before deciding whether to buy or not. They are most likely to develop more interest in the car and will end up buying it.

7. **The question close:** the focus of every good salesman from the beginning of the sales process is to close the sale as soon as possible. One good way to do this is to ask probing questions. These questions create and direct the flow of the conversation. By asking questions, the salesman gets to know the cause of objection from the prospect and answers accordingly. The more of their objections that you answer, the more interest you develop in the prospects for the product. These questions can also be used to close the sale. You can know when you have successfully cleared all

of their doubt by asking a question. *"Do you think that our product would be a good fit based on your company's policies?"* if you get a yes to a question like this, then you know that all that's left is to close the deal. You can use the same questions format to push for the close. *"Why do you think we shouldn't wrap this deal up now?"* the prospect will have just one answer to this question. *"Nothing let's wrap it all up then."* There you go, they sign on the dotted line and you have your sale.

8. **Suggestion close:** this close is a potent tool especially for those salesmen that are viewed as experts by the customers. If it's a new prospect, you can display enough expertise during the sales process that the prospects unconsciously begin to view you as an expert (you should be an expert of whatever you sell anyway). This close takes advantage of this expertise to help the prospect make the decision to buy. An example of this is; *"based on the situation of the market and my experience with other users of this product, I suggest you buy the three different types and try them out, it'll be easy for you to decide which one you prefer that way. All three are good but individual difference means you might prefer one to the others. Market situations also mean that they are not always readily available. I'll suggest you buy all three now that you have*

them and then focus later on the one you prefer." This sounds a lot like an expert opinion than a salesman trying to make a living. The prospect is more likely to believe you and buy all three. That means you'll be selling all three.

9. **Backward close:** this is a very unique and different type of close technique. It is called backward close because it closes the deal at the beginning of the deal. It requires a great deal and skill and expertise and is therefore not advisable for all salesmen. How this works is by asking the clients for referral even before you get to tell them a lot about your product. It's more like reversing the cycle. Remember that in having sales conversation, building rapport is very important. This technique can be used with a prospect after you have established rapport with them. Ask for a referral to their friends, families, and associates. It would most likely take them by surprise seeing that they don't really know much about the product. But they are enjoying the flow of the conversation and their rapport with you. Technically you're becoming their friend. They have a moral obligation to do a friend's first favor, so it's unlikely that they turn you down outrightly. What they'll do is ask to know about the product because if they are going to make a referral, their integrity is at stake. From here, you'll lecture them

extensively about the product. They will definitely listen keenly and this will build their interest. You must ensure you suggest to them to buy the product and test it for themselves. They definitely will buy it for two reasons, one, because they want to oblige your request for referral. Secondly, because their integrity is at stake so they" like to be sure of what they want to refer.

This is a small list of closing techniques, there are quite a number of them. The importance of closing a deal is the reason behind the different closing techniques that sales professionals have come up with. As a salesman, it's your duty to know your clients and know which particular close technique will work for them. You should as well know your stronger points and also know the close technique that you can use best. Some certain closing techniques require some skills and expertise than the others, so it's advisable that you stick to the closing technique that your skill, expertise, and level of experience allows you to engage. I wouldn't expect a rookie salesman to opt for the hard close, urgency close or even the backward close. However, the assumption close, summary close is good for starters.

There is no point in starting a sales conversation if you will not be able to close the deal. This doesn't mean that you will be successful in winning over every deal but the best salesmen are known for their ability to close deals. You should remember that the more deals you are able to close, the more sales you will make and the more income you get. If you can't close more deals, then you'll make minimal sales. To boost your sales is to increase your close rate.

Tips to increase your close rate

1. **Know your product:** this is very vital if you are really going to increase your sales. it is when you have a thorough knowledge of your product that you would be able to focus more on all the benefits it offers the customer. This means that you are more likely to understand your customer's pain point and explain to them how your product provides a solution to their problem. Many prospects know very well what they want to buy, so when you have not taken the time and pain to know your product well enough, there's no way you can convince them to buy from you even if what you are selling is what they need. Once the customer

knows the product than you do, they find it easy to dismiss you as a clueless salesman. This is in no way good for your reputation.

2. **Listening is an art that you have to learn:** when you do too much talking, you will learn a lot less about the prospect and their desires and pain points. This will invariably mean that you'll be clueless as to how to help them. In a sales conversation, the prospect is to do most of the talking. At least 70% of the talking should be done by the prospect. The more they talk, the easier it is for you to know them and how to sell to them and the easier it is to close the sale. When you give the prospect enough room to talk and express themselves, the more room you get to apply a variety of closing techniques to close the deal. During the sales conversation, make sure that your talk is minimal. Whenever you do talk, ensure that you're asking a question to drive the conversation further or you're agreeing with something they said. This gives them the confidence to keep talking. Don't make a habit of disagreeing a lot with the prospect. The more you disagree with them the more they lose confidence in their talks and

the sales process. As long as it doesn't compromise your sales standard, you don't have to let them know about your objections. Its either you listen to their objections in other to close the deal or they lose to your objections and call off the deal.

3. **Ask an open-ended question:** there is no worse way to destroy a conversation than to repeatedly ask the yes or no questions. They stiffen the flow of conversation. They are a no go area in a sales conversation. Take for instance,

- Salesman: do you want me to show you the product?

  Prospect: yes, please

  Salesman: will you like me to unpack this for you?

  Prospect: no, thank you.

  You will never be able to close any deal if you have a sales conversation in this manner. You'll be boring and you won't be able to learn anything from the prospect. Instead, you should ask open-ended questions that will make them talk and explain. This gives you the possibility of knowing their business problem and possible solutions to them. It'll be easier for you to close the deal if they see that you understand their pain point and you can offer the solution.

4. **Make sure you answer all their questions:** during sales conversation, as much as you ask the clients open-ended questions just to keep them talking for you to determine their desires and pain points, the prospects also want to get to know you. They want to know about your company and what you do there. They want to know how much you know about what you sell. They want to grade your degree of expertise. They want to be convinced that the product is actually right for them before they commit themselves to buy it. That is why they also ask you questions. The same way you ask them open-ended questions to know about them. The same applies to them too. They ask because they also seek answers to a lot of things. It would be wrong and unethical for you to ignore any of those pressing questions that they ask. Don't even try to wave away their questions with something else. Don't try to deflect the question. Nothing is more important to them at that time than the response they expect to get from you. You must ensure that you answer their questions very

adequately. Do the same thing you expect from them. Talk broadly, let them get to know about you from you. Don't hold back anything in answering their questions. The more of their questions that you answer, the more they get to know you. The more they get to know you, the more they get to trust you. The more they trust you, the easier they feel trying to do business with you. Don't forget the golden sales rule "people only buy from people that they trust." The more of their question that you deflect and fail to answer, the less confidence you inspire. They feel insecure more easily this way and you won't have their trust. Invariably they won't feel free to do business with you.

5. **Choose your words carefully:** the first point of sales is communication. Selling anything starts with communication between the seller and the buyer, this is what leads to a financial transaction. It is very necessary to be circumspect in your choice of words as well as how you say what you say. There's an impression that comes with every word and tonality of the words. In other to successfully pull the deal off, you must be careful to not give a false impression of yourself in your words and tone.

There are some words and phrases that shouldn't be in the vocabulary of a salesman. Words like maybe, I'm not sure, I think, I might, probably etc. generally, these are words that do not depict assurance and certainty especially when you use them for yourself or your company or your product. They don't inspire confidence in the prospect. You will find it hard to close any deal if the prospect hears too many of these words too often. They'll lose trust and confidence in you easily. There are however other words and phrases that the salesman should be heard regularly and constantly from the salesman. They should form the very basic core of his vocabulary. Words and phrases that fall into this category will be definitely, certainly, I assure you, you can rest assured etc. these are words and phrases that inspire confidence. It gives the prospect a sense of safety and security and assurance. They feel more at ease doing business with you as you confidently roll out these words.

6. **Keep your credibility intact:** your credibility as a salesman is not something you should toil with. Don't in the name of convincing a customer lie or over promise on

something that you cannot deliver on. Don't do anything that will taint your reputation. Make yourself and your brand referable. It's easier for you to close future deals if the customers trust you. They can also refer you to others who will view you the same way that they view you. This makes your work as a salesman easier. You increase your customer base, close more deals and make more sales simply by being credible.

7. **Research your prospect beforehand:** the internet is a very powerful tool for a salesman if they can use it wisely. All of your prospects have their profiles on different platforms on the internet. Go through it and try to know about them before you call them or meet them in person. It makes it easier for you to know what directions to channel the conversation. LinkedIn is a good way to know about your prospects. The time you invest in trying to know them will definitely pay off when you start the sales conversation.

Dealing with Objections – Please Prove that You Are Telling the Truth

Objections are a part of the sales process. It is very unlikely that you go through the whole sales process and sales conversation without having to deal with any objections from the prospect. It can't be that you're too good, it means your prospect is a dummy, you should run from them.

Objections are a tool in the hands of the prospect to try to make it hard for the deal to be brokered or to even ensure, as much as possible, that they don't make the purchase. However, this can turn out to be a very potent tool in the hands of a skilled, experienced and well-prepared salesman to ensure that they make the sale. It can be both a positive and a negative tool depending largely on how you deal with it.

For the salesman, objections are a good thing if they are discovered during the course of the conversation by asking appropriate questions. To deal with objections is to treat them as informative tools to know about the prospects, the thoughts running through their minds, their desires and pain points. The best way to manage objections is to treat them as information about the customer. If objections are incurred by the salesman, that's a bad sign. The point of probing the prospects is to find out about them, you're to find out the objections in them and to create one in them. If they have objections induced by talking to you, it will be difficult for you to close the deal, it could be a turn off for them. This self-incurred objection can be caused by being too pushy and forward and being too eager to close the deal. It can make them doubt your authenticity and that of your product.

Objections are what many sales prospect use to call off a deal with an inexperienced salesman. Many inexperienced salesmen spend a lot of time preparing and perfecting their sales pitch and they spend little or no time at all preparing for how they will handle objections posed by the prospects. Many of them will hope that the prospect doesn't have an objection, which is not possible. So they tend to be caught out unawares by their ill-preparedness and they end up losing the prospect because of a silly objection. In all my years as a salesman, I've come to realize that sales pitch don't win over a prospect as much as properly dealing with their objections does. This will mean that the bulk of preparation time before meeting a prospect should be spent on how to handle likely objections that you may encounter. This is what does more of the work in convincing the prospect.

To be able to deal effectively with objections, you have to know some of the reasons why the prospects object. The prospect will object for some of the following reasons;

1. They are skeptical about buying your product or buying from you: this means that they are not sure that your product is exactly what they need or they are not sure that you are the best person to sell it to them. This can happen when there's a lack of rapport between you and the prospect. When a salesman tries to just sell and not make any effort to build a relationship or rapport with the customer, this will create some kind of skepticism. It would make you appear pushy even if you don't mean to be pushy. A basic rule of the sales process is to genuinely listen to the prospect with keen interest. When they see how interested you are in them, they will reciprocate that by being interested in you and your product.

   Another reason for skepticism is when you don't ask the right questions or you ask them improperly. Running a sales conversation like an FBI interrogation will only put them on the defensive and they won't be in a position to buy from you. During sales conversation, you must be careful what you say to the prospect if you are going to make promises, make sure that they are achievable and attainable ones. You don't want the prospect thinking that you are only sweet talking them in other to get them to buy your product.

2. Miscommunication: it is the work of the salesman to ensure that all that he says to the prospect is well understood. The salesman must also ensure that he understands the prospects very well. This is the building block for making sales. it is practically impossible to complete a transaction when there's a lack of understanding or miscommunication between the buyer and the seller. You must ensure you ask questions for clarity in the case where you don't understand what the prospect is saying. You should also ask if you're understood and be willing to go over whatever you have said for clarity sake. The best way to avoid misunderstanding is to ensure that there's a right balance between listening and talking on both ends.

3. They might just be stalling: many at times, prospects object simply because they want to avoid making a decision at the

time. There are different reasons why prospects stall in the sales conversation. It may be because they are actually not in a position to make the decision. This happens especially if you're dealing with a representative from a company with a multi-level decision-making system. They might be convinced themselves but they don't just have the power to make the decision. It may as well be due to other available options. If you are talking to a prospect and they are stalling, for this reason, it means that you are not doing a good enough job of convincing them. Try harder. If they are not convinced about your product, rather than object immediately, they might stall while they seek other alternatives. Another important reason why prospect stall is that they can't afford the product at the moment. No matter how convinced a prospect is if they can't afford the product they won't buy it. It would just be one of the things on their wish list. It may mean that you are dealing with the wrong prospects for your business or you have to fit your price to their budget. If you can, try to be flexible with the payment option, offering them installment payments, in this case, might help out.

Other reasons why prospect objects;

- They don't like the product you are offering.
- They feel you are not listening well enough to them.
- The product they want to buy is very important to them and they can't afford to not get the best available in the market.
- They don't trust you.
- They are not interested or you are not saying something that interests them.

Many salesmen need to change their view about objection in other to properly deal with it. You must be able to see objections as opportunities to convince the prospects rather than a hindrance to making the sale.

If you are going to win over a customer that objects, one of the things that you must do very importantly is to agree first with their objection. I know what it sounds like if you agree to their objection, it means that's the end of the sale. This is the common mindset of the average salesman but it's not actually true. By agreeing first to their objection, you put yourself in a position to empathize with them and they see this. This makes them feel understood and shows that all along you have been listening to them.

You must take note that I said you should agree FIRST with their objections, I didn't say you should agree with them. That's the difference between the end of the sales process and finding a solution that ensures the sales process doesn't stop there.

When the prospects object, don't object to their objections. This creates an obvious impasse in the sales process. Responding with a "no, we can't do that" or a "that's a wrong step to carry". Responding in this manner creates a breach in communication between both parties. It makes them feel they're in the wrong place. The better way to respond is to acknowledge their objections. Every salesman must know that objections are a natural part of sales conversation and must welcome them as they come. A good response will be "okay, I understand what you mean", this acknowledgment makes them feel more relaxed. As a matter of fact, it will make them more attentive to you. They will become more interested in how you intend to solve that problem. You must realize that every time a prospect raises an objection, there's a little bit of tension in the air especially if the objection is monetary. It might be you who's feeling it or them or both of you.

This is why creating a little distraction after an objection might be a good idea. You can talk about sports or the weather for about two minutes. Look for a common ground between you both that isn't related to sales and money. This reduces the little tension in the air, then you can go back to the objection and try to deal with it. Make sure you don't overdo this, however. If you distract them from the objection for too long, it might give them the impression that you are shying away from it and this could be a huge turn off from them. You must ensure that the sales conversation continues even after they object. This will mean that you offer them a way to deal with that objection. As long as you can get the objection off the way, you have a prospect ready to buy your product.

Steps for handling objections

In handling objections, there are few steps that work very well. Understanding these steps and applying them are sure ways to deal with objections.

1. **Research your lead or prospect:** I have lost count of how many times that I have mentioned this in this book. That shows how important this is. When you have sufficient information about your prospect before meeting

with them it gives you a template with which to relate to them. Not researching them or not having a piece of prior knowledge about your prospect before a sales call or sales meeting leaves you blank and clueless about how to relate with them, what interests them, how to flow with the discussion etc. you are no different from a student that is going for an exam without reading. They'll be clueless about how to tackle the simplest question. That's direct access to an F. Researching the prospect already helps to reduce the number of objections that you hear during the sales conversation. It also prepares you to know how to properly answer or handle their objections.

2. **Pay attention to their concerns:** every salesman should know that objections raised during sales conversation are very valid and legitimate and should be treated as such. By listening to your clients closely during the sales conversation, you can determine what the cause of the objection is. This can help you to mine out their hidden pain points and desires. This allows you to hit the nail on the head. Nothing impresses a prospect more than a seller knowing stuff about them without them having to

say anything. Listening to understand the prospect is very important. Combative listen, when you are listening simply with the aim to give a response, a defense or an objection does not help to encourage a sale. Rather, you'll discourage the prospect. It will be obvious that you're not being attentive and this is a very potent way of killing the sales process. It is only by listening attentively that you can know the right response to give to their objections.

3. **Say the objection back to them:** this is a psychological kick back. After they have told you their objection. It is a good idea for you to take a while. Take a few seconds out to try to understand properly the objection that they raised. Then try to say it back to them. You can even rephrase it. For example;

Prospect: you have a nice product but I don't think it's worth the price you're naming. (The objection that is raised here is the price).

Salesman: …. (Takes some few seconds to think) I understand you very well sir. You like the product but the reason you aren't purchasing it is because you think it is expensive.

Prospect: that's exactly what I'm saying.

What this technique does is that it buys their attention. It opens up the path for you to tackle their objection while they listen to you attentively. It is easy for you to convince a prospect if you have their full attention. This is because they tend to reason along with you as you tackle their objections and they are more likely to see reason with you than not. It could also cause them to make a commitment. The scenario above is an example of that. The salesman says the reason the prospect is not buying is because they think it is expensive and the prospect agrees. This implies that if the salesman can overcome the price barrier, the prospect is committed to buying. Whether this is what the prospect intended with their objection is no longer very important. This step can also be used to portray your knowledge and expertise. If you are able to read back and explain their objections to them with clarity. The prospects will likely see you as a salesman with a knowledge of how their industry. This attracts them to you and makes them listen to you.

4. **Face the objection squarely:** this is the most obvious and important part of the steps. The reason for the previous three steps is because of this step. If you carry out the first three very well and flop at this, you still lose the clients. The other three are to help you with this. Imagine having to invest hours trying to research a prospect, only to get in front of them and you can't deal with their objection. Why waste all that time? Imagine after paying attention to all the prospects have to say and following along keenly and you can't answer the simple question they raised. You shouldn't even be speaking to them then. Why lay down the marker trying to understand their objection ad rephrasing it, trying to show your expertise, getting them to listen to you and at the end you don't have anything to say? Why waste everybody's time?

To face their objections squarely means that you have precise answers to their questions. It means that you have a solution that solves their problem and the objection that they have raised. You should know that you are not the first salesman they are having the same conversation with. They are likely not a startup company, meaning that they already have a solution and only want to know how yours differ from the one they have and if it's an upgrade on what they already have. This means that you have to know your product well and how it solves their problem.

Now you must ensure that you pass across your solution in simple, clear terms. Pick your words well. Don't use ambiguous words that will confuse them or make them misinterpret what you're saying. Make sure you're well understood. You can even ask them a question to see if they really understood you and if they share your view about how your product is their solution. You must be bold and confident about your product. Before you begin to answer their objection, ask them if they will buy the product once you can allay their fears. This would be demanding some commitment from them and if you are successful in convincing them, then they'll have no choice but to buy the product.

5. **Move on to the sale (close the deal):** after you have tackled the objection and you are sure that the prospects understand. There's no need for further ado, the next step is to ask for the sale. If you have done a good job in

convincing them and tackling their objection, they'll likely make the purchase. If they do, then you win. But if they say no, there are a few reasons for this. It could be that;

- They have other objections that you need to tackle. This means that the sales process has not ended.
- You did a poor job in tackling the objection.
- The prospect is a complete waste of time and not someone who can do a deal.

Typically, the end of a sales conversation is when the prospect buys the product (which is the aim of the whole sales process) or when you couldn't reach a compromise befitting for both parties and the deal is called off. If the reason they said no is because they have other objections, it means that you have to start the process of handling the objection all over again from the second step. You won't stop until you have totally tackled all their objections. Then it will result in a sale except they have another reason apart from other objections.

If the prospect says no because you didn't handle the objection well, there are two possibilities. They either give you a second chance, an opportunity for you to go over it again, which you must grab with both hands and make the most of its use. The second possibility is that they dismiss the deal, I which case you have to move on. The sad part of being a salesman is that you can't win every prospect and you have to learn to not sulk on a lost deal but focus on the ones you have at hand and getting others. If the prospect doesn't give you a second chance, it may be because they are just impatient or you don't sound convincing and are undeserving of another opportunity. A good salesman always ensures that the cause of objections and why the deal is going to be called off doesn't come from their end.

The prospect might as well say no because they are not worthy of this. You must learn quickly that not all prospects can become customers, many just are not cut out for what you sell. Don't down sell yourself, look for prospects and customers that are befitting of you and your product. Don't waste your time with people that can't do a deal.

Common types of objections that salesmen face

1. **The price objection:** when prospects use the price of your product as an objection, in many cases, the money is not the issue. The problem is that they are not convinced enough to pay. You have to show them why they should invest their money in your product and they'll gladly buy it. However, this is not true in every case. There are some prospects that actually don't have the money. There are some that cannot truly afford your product. Prospects like this will tend to ask for a discount on the price of the product. You don't have to sell yourself short. If they can't afford it, don't waste time trying to convince them. Look for a prospect that can pay for the product and invest your time in convincing them rather than waste your time on those that can't buy.

2. **The time objection:** this is another very common form of objection. When the prospects use time as the basis for their objection, it simply means that they are not yet ready to buy. Prospects often say things like

   "Send me an email with more information and I will get back to you"

   "I need you to give me some time to think about it."

"I will contact you later."

"Now is not a good time to talk, let's talk later."

When you get these objections, don't just hang up the call or end the meeting and start waiting for them to get back to you. The truth is they might never get back to you, especially if you sit idle and wait for them to come. Ask them open-ended questions immediately. This will reveal to you if the time objection is genuine or they are just not interested in your product. Asking a question like "is there any concern in particular that you will like me to address?" or "when should we schedule our next meeting." This affirms your interest in the prospect and gives you a chance to follow up on them. You don't give up on clients because of timing, except they have shown to be uninterested in your product and used the time as a cover to end the call or meeting. Ideally, the timing might be wrong but the sales can still go on at a later, more convenient time for the prospect. That's why following up on the prospect is important. It shows that you have them in mind and allows them to keep you in mind.

3. **The need objection**: this is the part of the sales conversation where prospects tell you that they don't need your product as a solution. This is a relatively easier objection to deal with than the first two. This is because this has more to do with you. Here the ball is in your court and all you need to do is show them that you're what they need. Let them see the difference between what they have at the moment and what you are offering to them. Show them how your product is an upgrade on what they currently have or use. Everybody tries to get better at each opportunity. If you can show them how you make them better, you will win them over. If they don't see what you offer as a priority, they will likely tell it to your face that you're not a priority. This means that you have been pitching wrongly. Your sales pitch have not been directed towards their desires and pain point. This is usually the result when a salesman goes through a sales conversation without researching the prospect to know more about their desires and priorities. There's no blanket sales conversation that works for all. Different prospects have their different selling points that's why you have to

painstakingly take the time to research each prospect. This will help you during the conversation.

4. **The trust objection:** some prospect might be skeptical about your company for many reasons mostly due to their previous experience with others. There's no telling the role that trust plays in closing a deal. As a salesman, it is your duty to win their trust for them to buy your product. When prospects tell you that they don't want to commit to your product because they don't trust you just yet, this is a window for you to tell them more about your company and what you do. Most importantly make sure you mention the names of other clients that you deal with especially if they are big guns, show them public positive reviews about you. This would help in convincing them. This is apart from building rapport with them that tends to win their trust as well.

5. **The authority objection:** this is the kind of objection where prospects tell you that they are not the one calling the shots In this case, what you'll do is ask to be redirected to the appropriate person. Tell them to help you set up a meeting with whoever is in charge or those that have the

power to make the sale. This means you'll have to go over everything again when you meet whoever is in charge and you have to be more impressive than the first time. This will take some preparedness on your side but in the end, it is worth it. The advantage of this approach is that if you successfully convince their rep and he sets up a meeting with the authority, the reps will stick it out for you to ensure they make the purchase.

6. **The competition objection:** this is when the prospect tells you that they are already dealing with your direct competition. What you'll do in this case is to ask them to follow up questions to determine the level of their satisfaction with your competition. Asking a question like "why did you opt for the service? What has working with them been like?" prospect that is not satisfied with the competition will be more willing to tell you about it, partly to see how you can do better. This is your chance. Look out for loopholes, weak spots, features that they might be missing out on that you can offer. Let them know what you bring to the table and how you are going to help them improve. Note that picking out weak spots in your

competition's offer is so that you can prove to them that you offer better and they can have a better experience with you. It's not to try to tear apart your competition in front of your prospect. That's classless and shows how desperate you are. It's definitely a good way to convince the prospect that you are not what they need.

Upselling – Getting the Biggest Commission from Every Lead

Upselling is a simple sales technique that encourages the buyer to buy more than they originally intended to buy. It would mean that the buyer buys a product at a more expensive price. It is a technique that allows the seller to make more profitable sales by influencing the buyer to buy the more expensive upgraded or the premium version of whatever product that they desire. It may also be to make more sales by selling additional goods or service to the customer.

Upselling is mutually beneficial to both the buyer and the seller. Although it means that the customer will spend more (which benefits the seller), the buyer spending the money will be getting a good value for their money.

Upselling is a very important part of many business models. It is how many models get most of the profit from their sales revenue. Upselling existing customers is known to be 5-10 times cheaper than getting new customers. It is a low-risk sales technique that allows the salesman to make their sale with minimal effort. It, therefore, becomes a very important part of the sales strategy. In starting up and growing your business, you must make sure that you plan strategically for upselling. This will go a long way in generating more income for you.

A very big advantage of upselling apart from the higher profits that you get is that you get to retain your customers. It has been proven that customers who buy more from you are more likely to come back to you. Upselling doesn't just improve your profits margin, it also increases your customer retention. As long as the quality of your products remain and customers are pleased with your upsell, you'll be building a long lasting and loyal fan base for yourself.

How to upsell your customers

1. **Offer only relevant upsell to the product that the customer wants to buy:** this would mean that if you're offering additional products as an upsell to the customer's desired product, whatever you add must be relevant to what they want. For example; if you go to the cinemas, apart from whatever price you have to pay to see the movies, they have stands where they sell popcorns. Eating popcorns is very much associated with seeing moves at the cinemas that if they don't have popcorn, you would likely feel cheated and the movie might not interest you as such. You tend to forget that you have to pay extra fees to buy that popcorn. That's an upsell. They make you buy something very much relevant to what you want, meaning

you have to pay for more than just what you want. I'm sure you must have come across this phrase "upgrade to premium". It's the same thing that many phone applications and sites do when they ask you to upgrade to premium. The premium package has a lot of benefits than the basic package and this tempts you to invest your money in it. Upselling can offer as much as 30% of a business profit. If everybody in a cinema were to buy a pack of popcorn each, think how much the cinema would make from selling popcorns alone in one night apart from the profits they make from showing the movie itself. Adding relevant offers is very important to making upsell. The reason this works perfectly is because of the connection between the original product they are purchasing and the additional product that you are upselling. When you try to upsell a product that doesn't relate with the original product that they purchased, it can appear that you are trying to squeeze out more money from them than they are ready to let go off. this is very likely to turn them off and you might end up losing your credibility with the customer and the customer themselves. But when you upsell a product as an add-on as in the examples above, the customer feels like you're trying to improve their experience with their purchased product. They will gladly go for the upsell and thank you for it.

2. **Make the upsell at a discounted price:** when you offer an upsell to a customer, the first thing they think of is the price. They begin to think, how much it will cost them, whether or not they can afford it. If you make your upsell such that it is expensive, it will be difficult for the customer to go for it. You can make the upsell half of the price of their initial purchase or even less. They'll be more willing to buy if they can evidently see the price gulf between their original product and your additional product and yet both product complement each other well. Never give them the impression that the upsell is expensive, instead, let them see it as an opportunity to not pass by. For instance, if they buy a product for $100, you can offer them an upsell at $40 or $50. They will naturally be forced to think of the importance of enjoying their initial product. Seeing that it is cheap will help them make the decision to buy it as well. After all, if they can buy this for $100, $40 shouldn't be

much of a problem for them. That'll be their mindset as well. If you want to make a higher upsell or an expensive upsell, you can make the payment more flexible. This will ease the price burden and give them an illusion that it is not expensive.

For example:

Salesman: would you like me to add Product B as well?

Customer: (the first thing they consider is the price) ... how much does it cost?

Salesman: you can get it for as low as $15 per month for 6 months.

To sum that up, it's a total of $90 but the customer doesn't hear that. What they hear is the cheap $15 to be paid monthly. This is however not advised. Upselling is about having quick wins. So it is safer to stick to that. You should look to sell low priced, relevant additions during upsell. It is not likely that the customer buys a product of $100 and an additional one at $90. The probability is low. You should ensure that the price between their original product and the additional product is about $60 off.

3. **Don't jump the gun:** one common mistake I've seen many salesmen make in the process of upselling is that they offer the upsell before the customer buys the original item. For many customers, this is likely to turn them off. Nobody likes it when prices are suddenly increasing on them. They begin to feel you're exploitative and might as well not buy anything at all. Instead, wait till they have checked out on their original purchase and then offer the upsell. At this point, it is clear to them that they want what they wanted at the normal price. They don't think you're trying to exploit them, they'll rather think that you're trying to help them enjoy fully the product they have purchased. This will inspire them to make a second purchase. This time for the upsell.

4. **Sell products in their pairs:** the reason why many customers make purchases is that they want to solve a particular problem. The purchased item, however, could end up being a problem or creating another problem for the customers. For example, a customer buys a rug to beautify their floor. After laying the rug, the initial problem is solved, the floor is now beautiful. However, the rug is

going to get dirty and suck up dust. This is another problem on its own. The customer will need a vacuum cleaner to solve that problem. This means they have to make another purchase. It would be wise for you as a salesman to not just sell rugs that solve a problem to create another. Sell the solution to the problem it solves as well. In this case, a vacuum cleaner. This will enable you to upsell the vacuum cleaner whenever anyone wants to buy a rug. They're most likely to buy both at a time due to the stress of having to look for vacuum cleaner later and the extra cost it might incur. This means more sales for you as a salesman and more income as well. Whatever product you sell, if you plan to upsell as well, make sure you sell the solution to the problem it creates as well. This might require you to think carefully about your product and try to highlight the problem it creates and other product that can solve them.

5. **Offer assurances:** offering assurances to prospects and customers is a big part of the sales process.it many times determine whether or not the sale will go through. In making an upsell, it is even more important because you're

not just selling one product but two. To get the customers off their guards at the mention of an upsell will require you offer plenty of assurances and guarantee about the products you're selling. This put your credibility at stake but you must be able to eliminate the idea in the mind that buying your upsell is a risk. Once you can achieve this, there's a very high possibility that you will be successful with the upsell.

6. **Show the value:** many people are willing to spend their money on products only if they are sure of how valuable the product is to them. The same goes with upselling a product. It's not enough that you have made recommendations on the said products as additions. You must be able to show the value of the product to the customer. This makes them more relaxed and puts them in a better frame of mind to buy the additional product. They won't see it as an opportunity for you to make more money. They would rather see it as an opportunity for them to get more value for and from the product they are buying.

It is important in upselling to make the customer see that you're trying to help them and not just trying to make more money for your own self. Having this view of you will not help you convince them to make the purchase.

Two basic rules of upselling are these;

1. Never sell to an angry customer: if you have a customer who doesn't seem to be happy with your product or service, the solution would not be to offer them an upsell. That'll be insane. You want them to buy more from you when you have not made any efforts to pacify their anger. Upselling should never be an option to angry, upset or disappointed customers. Rather than try to make them buy more. You should focus your energy on what they are not happy with your product or service and try to help them solve the issue. Once you have successfully pacified them, upselling would not be an issue. The easiest way to lose a customer is to try to upsell to them when they are disappointed at you. It turns them off. it portrays you as a selfish salesman, one who only cares about having more sales and making more money and doesn't give a damn whether or not the customers are satisfied. You must ensure that your customers are happy with your previous services before suggesting an upsell with them. Already you have

credibility with them so it makes it easy for you to make the upsell.

2. Make sure the upsell pitch paints the customers as the winner: a popular sales quote from Jeffrey Gitomer is this; "tell me how I win. When I win, you win." This is a simple and very applicable principle. If the customers see themselves as the winners of your up sale, if they think that it benefits them more and you're only trying to help them, there is nothing that would stop them from making the purchase. Once they make the purchase, you win. You must ensure, as much as possible, that you carry out your sales process and upselling in a customer-first manner. You must ensure you're not being pushy about the deal as it makes them feel you're doing it for yourself.

Common examples of upselling

1. **Dollar shave club:** this brand lures people with their cheap initial offer (which also happens to be their brand name) then they provide two other options that gives much more value than the basic one dollar option. These other two options tend to interest you more than the original standard option that attracted you. This means that if you

are going to leave the initial one dollar option for either of the other juicier options you will have to pay more. This is a perfect example of upselling. The customers are more willing to pay more to get better features than the one dollar offer and they are happy to do so. Remember that in upselling, it should always be a win-win situation. You win when the customer pays more and the customer wins when they get more value from the product.

2. **Spotify:** comparing two different options of a product side by side will always expose the inadequacies in the features of one and the excellence in the features of the other. This will automatically make one more desirable than the other. This is the technique that Spotify uses. Spotify writes out the 6 features of their product on both the free option and the premium option. The premium option has access to all of these 6 features while the free option has access to just one of the features. If all you knew was the free option and its feature, you won't know how much you are missing out. That's why they put both options side by side. Looking at the free option with one feature and the premium with all 6 features makes the free option undesirable (even though it

is free), the experience that you can have with all the 6 features is all you start to think about and you really will desire it. What you might not remember here is that the additional 5 features come with a price. But buyers will be ready to pay that price just to have a better experience using the product. Now that's upselling.

3. **Amazon:** if you have ever purchased anything on Amazon, then you should be familiar with this phrase "frequently bought together". This is a recommendation that Amazon makes based on what you buy. They suggest related items for you and most times customers tend to find another product that they have to buy but had skipped their mind. For instance, if you buy a camera on Amazon, they could suggest a memory card as the "frequently bought together" recommendation. And you suddenly realize that you need space to save all your shots. So although you planned to buy just a camera, you ended up buying a memory card as well. In some cases, you could have up to three suggested products as "frequently bought together" recommendation and you're most likely to need all three as well as your initial good. So you end up buying 4 instead of just 1.

4. **BMW:** the BMW site actually allows their user to customize the car they intend to purchase before making the order. This gives the customer a chance to change and upgrade parts of the car from wheels, the seats and almost any part of the car can be changed or upgraded. However, each upgrade or change comes with a price. For instance, If a car is worth $500,000 and the buyer makes upgrades worth $50,000 on the car, that means he'll be paying for additional buys worth $50,000 instead of just the $500,000 for the car.

Conclusion

From the very first chapter of this book, you have seen the goal of this book clearly stated. This book aims at increasing the income of the salesman by massively boosting their sales through tested and tried techniques. This book seeks to educate the reader (which presumably is a salesman) on the different aspects of a sales process. Starting from things you do during the sales call or a sales meeting with the prospect, how you build rapport with them, how to handle qualifications, how to close a deal, how to handle objections, and upselling to a customer.

This chapter contains a detailed summary of what this book is all about on a chapter by chapter basis.

Chapter one – First impression is everything

This chapter explains how to open a sales conversation. The reason that many salesmen do poorly in sales conversations is because they lack good communication skills. If you are someone with a good enough communication skill, you wouldn't find it difficult to start a conversation or sustain one. But when you can't even start a conversation, how will you be able to sustain one? If you've read this paragraph well enough, you would have noticed that I have been using the word 'conversation' in the place of 'sales conversation'. Of course, this is a sales book and what I am definitely referring to is the sales conversation. I was intentional in removing the word 'sales', this is detoxify your mind from the usual thinking that sales conversation is different from the normal day to day conversation that we have with our friends, families and even strangers. I find it funny that some salesmen are free and flows very well during a "normal" conversation but struggles to keep up during a "sales" conversation. This keeps me wondering, "what's the difference?" as far as I know, they are both conversations. The only difference that I can think of is their emphasis. While the day to day conversation will center on different things going on in our individual lives, our common challenges, our goals and things we generally love and hate individually and collectively, the sales conversation, on the other hand, centers on business, sales, buying and selling. But that doesn't mean you can't be free to enjoy a sales conversation, it's your job, your duty. You should enjoy having a sales conversation as a salesman.

This chapter of the book teaches the salesman (especially the struggling one) how to open a sales conversation. There are different scenarios to which the conversation would need to be open. It could be a conversation through a sales call (where the salesman calls the prospect on the phone). It could be a sales meeting (where the salesman meets with the prospects in person to discuss the sales). Likewise, it could be that the customer walks through the doors into the store. Sales conversation in these 3 scenarios are opened differently and all the processes and tips to successfully open the conversation are well explained in this chapter.

Chapter two – Brush offs – how to get around every "it's not a convenient time"

This chapter basically explains how to convince the prospect to buy your product whether or not they have initially dismissed it. When the clients say "it's not a convenient time for a product", your reaction shouldn't be "okay, please check back on us whenever is convenient for you." The truth is there'll never be a convenient time to buy any product. So you don't have to give in to that excuse. Ideally, it just means that they are not interested in the product. Except you want to keep losing all your prospect, you must make sure that they don't hang up the call on you or end the meeting after saying that. Ensure that they stay a little bit longer on the call or at the meeting. This will afford you more time to convince them about the product. One way to do this is to ask an open-ended question. This gets their attention and they tend to keep them talking. The longer they get to talk, the longer the conversation gets and typically the more time you get to convince them about the product. Haven gotten their attention, there are six steps clearly explained that will help the salesman in convincing the prospect to buy the product. This will include you showing them the product. This is more effective for a sales meeting. Letting the customer see the product and have a feel of it tends to appeal to their emotions. Then you tackle their concerns heads on. Paint a picture of what their lives or companies will be like with your product in it. Offer them a guarantee on the product. This places your integrity and that of your company or brand at stake. If you can't offer a guarantee on what you are selling, you might as well not sell it at all. That means that there's no genuineness to what you are doing as a salesman. You must be able to offer assurances. The power of persuasion is a strong tool in the hands of a salesman. A good salesman should know how to persuade a buyer to buy their goods. As a matter of fact, you are only a salesman because you can persuade people to buy what you are selling.

Chapter 3 – Rapport – the lubricant of the system

Of course, the reason why we apply lubricant to machines and other things, in general, is to avoid friction and ensure a free flow of movement. This is true of rapport. The only way that sales conversation can flow is when there's a rapport between the salesman and the prospect. Rapport helps you to build a strong relationship. It is not new that relationships thrive on communication. Building rapport with your customers ensures that you have an interest in them and it as well builds interest on their side. There is a sales adage that "people only buy from people they like." If you have a reputation for being a frowning and unfriendly salesman, it's unlikely that you attract prospects to you and a lot more difficult for you to close a deal. It is easier for you to close a deal when the prospect trusts you and one of the fastest ways to build trust or to gain the prospect's trust is by having a strong rapport with them. This chapter has enough details on how to how to build rapport with your prospects. An important part of sales conversation as I explained is that it is not a lecture. The prospects will not just sit down and listen to you talk. It is a conversation, they are meant to be involved as well. You must give them the chance to talk. As a matter of fact, the prospect should do more of the talking. One very important skill that the salesman must cultivate is the listening skill. The salesman must be a very good and attentive listener, not just a talker. In fact, you'll be a better talker if you are an attentive listener. That's why the prospects should do about 70% of the talking. Be sure to quietly and attentively listen along. It is only when you listen attentively that you can understand the prospect point of view, their wants, needs, desire, pain points. It is only by listening attentively and keeping the conversation going by asking relevant questions and making suggestions that you will be able to draw all these out. Apart from this, it will give the prospect a worthy feeling of honor knowing that they are being listened to. Everybody wants to be understood and the only way you can understand a prospect is by listening to them when they talk.

Chapter 4 – qualification – people want to buy expensive things

One of the things you must realize early enough as a salesman is that not every prospect qualify to be your customer. In the sales process, you must be able to determine certain pointers during the conversation. Knowing these early enough will save you a lot of time, you'll be able to qualify whether the person you are speaking to is the ideal prospect for you. These pointers are; budget or spending power, authority to make a decision, revenue generation over time, the time frame for the sale, alternatives and requirements. It will be naïve on your part if you invest so many hours trying to convince a client who doesn't have the spending power to buy what you sell. No matter what you say, they just cannot buy it because they don't have the money even if they like it. This is not the kind of prospect you should meet with at all, how much more spend time trying to convince. It only deprives you of precious time that you would have invested in more profitable prospects. You must determine the type of customer that suits your product very early enough and see of each of the prospects you meet or talk to qualify to be one. If they don't, don't hesitate to let them go and go in search of your ideal customer. You have to be able to estimate your prospects and see if they meet your standard.

Another thing that this chapter considered is the requirement. Although this doesn't apply to every salesman, it's an important part of sales conversation for those it applies to. You must ask the prospect or customer if they are licensed by the law to be in possession of or to make use of your product (if you sell a product with legal barriers). For example, alcohols shouldn't be sold to minors. You must ask that customer or prospect how old they are to be sure they are not below 18 before you sell to them.

Chapter 5 – adding scarcity and urgency. Never hear again "call me tomorrow".

Adding scarcity and urgency to your sales is a sales technique that feeds on people's psychology and forces them to make an immediate purchase.

Scarcity refers to placing a limit on the amount of product supplied or a service rendered with the view of putting the customers or final consumers under pressure to buy. The goal behind creating scarcity is for the customers to feel the pressure and ultimate to boost sales of the particular product. Scarcity always creates a sense of urgency in the buyers. It is an effective way to boost sales rapidly.

The urgency that comes with scarcity is the reason why scarcity works. People who are known to sit on the fence about a particular product would be moved to make a quick decision. For instance, you most probably would have tried convincing a customer about a particular product without any luck. They might have appeared unconvinced or even very skeptical about the product. The moment they discover that it is already I'm short supply, you'll definitely notice a change in their appraisal of the product. They start having second thoughts, positive ones this time. The longer the scarcity, the more urgent people see the need for the product. Scarcity forces people to act immediately. Nobody likes to hear the statement "out of stock". That's why when a product becomes scarce, people do all they can to ensure that they have their share of the remaining lots before it's out of stock.

In this chapter, we also examined different ways to create scarcity in other to boost your sales. There are 4 ways to do this clearly explained in this book. Setting deadlines for product sales. This means giving a limited time offer for sales of particular products. Adding countdown for prices is also a time-bound scarcity. This tactic makes use of a reduction in the price of products to motivate people to buy within a small time scale. Holiday or seasonal offers is what you put up during a holiday or specially celebrated events. Use urgent words in your conversation. Words like instantly, immediately, right now, a limited number can be used to stimulate urgency in the prospect.

Chapter 6 – suggesting a close – closing smoothly

Closing a sale is the high point of any sales conversation. This is where you want all time, energy, resource and talks to end up at. If you talk for so long and it doesn't end up at closing a sale, it might as well have been a waste of time. This is the crux of sales meetings. This is the reason why you keep calling prospects, meeting with them to discuss, spend a lot of time trying to convince them to buy that good, it's all in a bid to close a sale. Closing a sale would generally refer to when the clients finally make the decision to buy your product or make the purchase. It is usually the end of the sales process.

Closing a deal really shouldn't be a big deal for a good salesman especially if he has done his homework well during the sales process. Closing the deal might be as simple as making just one statement or in many cases, just a suggestion. While in other cases, it might be as difficult as going over the whole sales process again. Suggesting a close during sales conversation is the duty of the salesman and should be the last on the agenda of things to do. Only 1 out of 10 prospects will be willing to close the sale by themselves so the onus is on the salesman to close the deal. You should only go for it after you are certain.

There is no point in starting a sales conversation if you will not be able to close the deal. This doesn't mean that you will be successful in winning over every deal but the best salesmen are known for their ability to close deals. You should remember that the more deals you are able to close, the more sales you will make and the more income you get. If you can't close more deals, then you'll make minimal sales. To boost your sales is to increase your close rate.

In this chapter, we explained about 9 sales closing techniques and also explained about different tips to increase your closing rate.

The assumption close, urgency close, hard close, puppy close, suggestion close, the backward close, take away close, summary close and the question close are the 9 closing techniques discussed in this chapter.

Chapter 7 – dealing with objections – please prove me that you're telling the truth

This chapter is about explaining what objections really are, how the salesman ought to view them. It was also well explained how they are to be handled and whether or not they are advantageous to the salesman and their chances of closing the deal. This chapter also deals with the reason why people object and the common objections that the salesman has to overcome.

Objections are a tool in the hands of the prospect to try to make it hard for the deal to be brokered or to even ensure, as much as possible, that they don't make the purchase. However, this can turn out to be a very potent tool in the hands of a skilled, experienced and well-prepared salesman to ensure that they make the sale. It can be both a positive and a negative tool depending largely on how you deal with it.

Objections are what many sales prospect use to call off a deal with an inexperienced salesman. Many inexperienced salesmen spend a lot of time preparing and perfecting their sales pitch and they spend little or no time at all preparing for how they will handle objections posed by the prospects. Many of them will hope that the prospect doesn't have an objection, which is not possible. So they tend to be caught out unawares by their ill-preparedness and they end up losing the prospect because of a silly objection. In all my years as a salesman, I've come to realize that sales pitch don't win over a prospect as much as properly dealing with their objections does. This will mean that the bulk of preparation time before meeting a prospect should be spent on how to handle likely objections that you may encounter. This is what does more of the work in convincing the prospect. The way we handle the prospect's objections often determines whether or not they will make the purchase.

Chapter 8 – upsell – getting the biggest commission from every lead

Upselling is a simple sales technique that encourages the buyer to buy more than they originally intended to buy. It would mean that the buyer buys a product at a more expensive price. It is a technique that allows the seller to make more profitable sales by influencing the buyer to buy the more expensive upgraded or the premium version of whatever product that they desire. It may also be to make more sales by selling additional goods or service to the customer. Upselling is mutually beneficial to both the buyer and the seller. Although it means that the customer will spend more (which benefits the seller), the buyer spending the money will be getting a good value for their money. In upselling, there is a win-win situation. The seller wins when the buyer pays more money than they intended and the buyer also wins by getting a better product than they wanted.

It has been proven that upselling to existing customers is about 5-10 times cheaper than looking for a new prospect. That makes upselling an important part of your business model, an art to be mastered.

In this chapter, 6 different steps were taught on how to upsell to a customer. Two basic rules of upselling were also explained. The first rule is to never sell to an angry customer. When a customer is not happy with your service or product, try to solve the issue with them first. Don't even think of upselling to them. The second rule is to pain the customer as the winner. "Tell me how I win. When I win, you win." You win I the customer buys the product thinking they are the winner. Well, it's a win-win situation.

I would find it impossible to believe that any salesmen who will read this book and implement the steps and tips in it, will not make more sales. Some of the things that are explained in this book might not be totally strange to you as a salesman. Many times, the reason even good salesmen don't close as much deals as they would have loved to maybe because of little tips that they overlooked. This book will help you to bring back that focus on those little things that can help boost your income through sales.

As long as you have read this book with a serious mind and not just another novel or piece of literature, you'll be able to take advantage of the information in it. With all the steps explained painstakingly in this book, if they are well followed, you should brace yourself for a massive sales boost.

We'll like to know what you think about this book. Your opinion is very important to me. So please, do well to review this book on Amazon.

Printed in France by Amazon
Brétigny-sur-Orge, FR